Longman

D0268178

York Press

York Press
322 Old Brompton Road, London SW5 9JH

Pearson Education Limited
Edinburgh Gate, Harlow, Essex CM20 2JE, United Kingdom
Associated companies, branches and representatives throughout
the world

First published 2000

ISBN 0-582-43200-6

Designed by Vicki Pacey
Phototypeset by Gem Graphics, Trenance, Mawgan Porth, Cornwall
Colour reproduction and film output by Spectrum Colour
Printed in Malaysia, KVP

contents

—///—

author of this note Mark Reid works in the Education Department of the British Film Institute. Prior to that he taught English, Media and Film at a college in south London.

CASABLANCA **y**

background

trailer

Here is a drama that lifts you right out of your seat. That Warners had a lucky break in the progress of world events that put the name of Casablanca on everyone's lips is the answer to the sure fire box-office smash the Hal B. Wallis production will enjoy.

The Hollywood Reporter, 8 December 1942

Much credit accrues to everybody connected with the production. Michael Curtiz, its director; Hal Wallis for the extent to which his production values reach; Arthur Edeson's matchless photography, music by Max Steiner and orchestral arrangements by Hugo Friedhofer, Julius and Phillip Epstein's and Howard Koch's screenplay ...

Variety, 8 December 1942

This brilliant production maintains the atmosphere of despair, hope, corruption and heat throughout. The direction is masterly, and the lighting and photography most effective. Humphrey Bogart is admirable as Rick, and Ingrid Bergman has about her a freshness and charm that is unusual.

Monthly Film Bulletin, January 1943

Casablanca, opening simultaneously at the Warner and the Regal this weekend, is a long and lively film, bulging with acting talent, and breathless with its own dramatic momentum ... Miss Bergman's noted beauty has never been so breathtaking, and she begins to act as well.

Today's Cinema, 15 January 1943

> Cinema par excellence: a studio bound Hollywood melodrama which after various chances just fell together impeccably into one of the outstanding entertainment pieces of cinema history, with romance, intrigue, excitement, suspense, and humour cunningly deployed by master technicians and a perfect cast.
>
> *Halliwell's Film and Video Guide, 1997 edition.*

reading casablanca

While writing this book I caught a glimpse of an episode of the soap opera *EastEnders*. A character, Terry, toasted his wife with a glass of champagne and the words 'Here's looking at you, kid'. Here was evidence that *Casablanca* has entered the popular imagination, and more, that its key lines have entered the language. This book is an exploration of the processes, choices, and accidents which have given *Casablanca* its pre-eminent position in film culture.

Casablanca is more than just a popular Hollywood film; it is a kind of touchstone – its central relationship signifies a type of powerful feeling, its central character a kind of heroic noble integrity, its central song exemplifies what Noel Coward called 'the potency of cheap music'. Overall it also signifies a kind of nostalgia – for codes and values which probably never existed except in the idealisations of the dream factory; 'you must remember this' as the old song puts it.

The film occupies a unique place in popular culture this century – it is both enormously popular and critically resisted. *Citizen Kane* (1941) is perennially the critics' favourite, along with the films of other noted 'auteurs' – Hitchcock, Renoir, Kurosawa – but *Casablanca* (and how many people can name Michael Curtiz as the director?) has a different kind of appeal, despite, maybe even because it is so corny. Billy Wilder called it the most marvellous claptrap.

Fifty years after it was released there was an orgy not of re-appraisal, but of celebration, all asking the same question – why has it retained its appeal?

The answer lies partly in its quotability – 'Here's looking at you, kid'; 'round up the usual suspects'; 'play it, Sam'; 'of all the gin joints in all the world she had to walk into mine'. It has provided the titles of other films – *Play it Again, Sam*; *The Usual Suspects*. The script crackles – but the lines have to be delivered – by Bogart ('The Germans wore grey, you wore blue'); Bergman ('Was that cannon fire, or the sound of my heart pounding?'); Claude Rains ('I'm shocked! Shocked to find gambling going on here!').

Legend has accrued around the shoot; Bergman didn't know who she would leave for Lisbon with; Bogart ad-libbed the most famous line; new script pages were delivered daily. There are apocryphal pre-production stories – Ronald Reagan and Ann Sheridan to star, composer Max Steiner thinking he could write something better than 'As Time Goes By'.

Its ambiguity – its indeterminacy – lies at the heart of its appeal. Do Rick and Ilsa sleep together when she visits his apartment? Why was Rick never allowed back to America? And as Umberto Eco asks, why does Laszlo, a famous Resistance hero, order three different drinks at Rick's bar?

The film is, as critic Andrew Sarris put it, the 'happiest of happy accidents'; this book tries to trace how this particular accident happened.

CASABLANCA – A BRIEF STORY

The film is based on a stage play called *Everybody Comes to Rick's*, which was never produced. Successive writers were set to work on converting it, some claiming that there is no resemblance between the film and the original play. This is far from the truth, however: the premise, the central character, many of the famous lines, and the ending were all in the original.

The project was taken on at Warner Bros by Hal B. Wallis, the powerful executive in charge of production; he saw in it an opportunity to capitalise on America's entry into the Second World War – both for commercial and patriotic reasons. The script landed on his desk on 8 December 1941, the day after the Japanese destroyed Pearl Harbor. He also saw it as a vehicle for the up-and-coming Humphrey Bogart who, at forty-two, was an actor being belatedly built into a star.

Michael Curtiz, a contract director who had learned his trade in Europe, and who could turn his hand to any material, was lined up to direct. He saw the first draft of the script in April 1942. The script itself was never really

typical for an A-feature

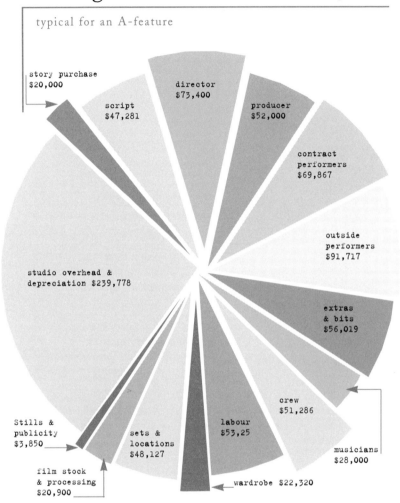

story purchase
$20,000

script
$47,281

director
$73,400

producer
$52,000

contract
performers
$69,867

outside
performers
$91,717

studio overhead &
depreciation $239,778

extras
& bits
$56,019

crew
$51,286

Stills &
publicity
$3,850

sets &
locations
$48,127

labour
$53,25

musicians
$28,000

film stock
& processing
$20,900

wardrobe $22,320

At just under $900,000, *Casablanca's* budget was typical for an A-feature in 1942, although it might have cost as much as $1,400,000 if it had been made at MGM instead of the notoriously frugal Warner Bros. *Casablanca's* director, Michael Curtiz, was paid over twice as much as any of the movie's stars, and the studio spent more on outside talent hired at weekly rates just for the movie than it did on the salaries of its contract players. Much of the cost of set construction, props, costume, and the like were absorbed in the 35% charge attached to the budget for the overheads in running the studio.

Source: adapted from Rudy Behlmer, ed., Inside Warner Bros (1935-1951), London, Weidenfeld and Nicolson, 1986

'finished', in common with studio practice. When shooting began on 25 May 1942, much of it was yet to be written. Re-drafts were produced daily, and even when the picture was complete, edited, and scored, Wallis was still making changes. The most famous was his idea for the last line of the film: 'Louis, this is the beginning of a beautiful friendship', for which Bogart had to be recalled to the studio to record.

Shooting the film took sixty days (ten weeks as even the studios rested on a Sunday), eleven days over schedule – which was about standard for a prestige film of the time – as was the budget at just under $900,000. A breakdown of the budget reveals the priorities – and the power distribution – in a Hollywood studio of the time. The rights to the original story cost $20,000, and the cost of scripting and rewrites was more than twice that.

Bogart was the most expensive performer, but pro-rata Sydney Greenstreet scored higher for his cameo appearance. Bergman and Paul Henreid cost the same, but their career trajectories were headed already in very different directions. Sets, locations, and wardrobe were budgeted at a relatively low $70,000; Warner Bros were notoriously the most frugal of the major Hollywood studios, and this was wartime.

Shooting finished on 3 August 1942. From here the picture was scored, edited, and dialogue was added, as well as new footage. Versions were screened for Jack Warner, head of production, and for the Warner Bros marketing machine. A print was hurriedly made ready to open in the Hollywood Theatre in New York, on Thanksgiving Day, 1942. The US Army had just landed in French Morocco, and the seaport city of Casablanca was on every newspaper front page.

The nationwide release was not until the following January. The cost of prints, marketing and promotion added another $150,00 to the budget; by the time the film completed its first run, it had taken over $3,000,000. Including overseas income, Casablanca made nearly $7,000,000 at the box office, which made it the third most successful Warner Bros film made during the war.

Casablanca was nominated for eight Academy Awards in 1944 – and it won three, for Best Screenplay, Best Director, and Best Picture. The Best

Picture Oscar was picked up by Jack Warner, in a moment that Hal Wallis felt should have been his. The resentment led almost immediately to the dissolving of their partnership.

key players' biographies

COMMUNITY OF ACTORS

More so than any contemporary film, *Casablanca* owes much of its impact to an ensemble of actors. Seventy-five actors have roles in the film, which gives it a human texture and feel of community that is absent in Hollywood films today. Current mainstream cinema has become over-reliant on the appeal of very big-name stars; the pleasures they offer occlude any more subtle portrayals of groups of people.

Rick's Café Americain, the major setting of *Casablanca*, is more than the bar owned by the lead male character; it is a kind of home to a large number of European refugees, whose communal spirits are raised by the music of Sam. In a sense, the bar is a metaphorical version of America for those very same actors.

Aljean Harmetz (1993) notes that only three of the thirteen actors given screen credit were born in America, and some twenty-five of the players were real refugees from Europe. Not only did the parallel between the film's scenario and the real-life experiences of these people add depth and texture to the drama, but so did the fact that many of them had been big stars in Europe, forced to turn their backs on their success for their own safety.

Marcel Dalio, Rick's flustered croupier, had starred in two Jean Renoir films, *La Grande Illusion* (1937), and *Le Regle du Jeu* (1939); Leonid Kinsky had been a big-name actor in St Petersburg and S.Z. Sakall similarly, a popular comedian in Hungary and later Germany. Many of them had had desperate passages from Europe to America, some as in the film, via Lisbon.

The bigger name actors had similar backgrounds: Conrad Veidt, for example, was the lead character in *The Cabinet of Dr. Caligari* (1919), a milestone in German Expressionist cinema, and Peter Lorre was the star of another, *M* (1931). Paul Henreid had been a member of the Austrian demi-aristocracy but fled the Nazis, eventually landing in America destitute.

With all this European baggage, it is hardly surprising that the crew who were on set during the singing of the 'Marseillaise' noticed that half of the cast were crying.

While the range and depth of characterisation give the film much of its power and texture, the burden of the drama is shared between five actors – Bogart, Bergman, Rains, Henreid, and Dooley Wilson. Of these, only two, Bogart and Bergman, could really be called stars, even though Peter Lorre, Rains, Henreid and Sydney Greenstreet were given featured billing on the screen credits.

The fact that Lorre and Greenstreet were given featured billing, while Dooley Wilson was not, even though Sam is a more important role, points to different levels of 'pull' in Hollywood. The disjunction between screen-time and billing, in both their cases, also suggests that they offered pleasures to an audience beyond their simple roles in the plot. In fact, Lorre and Greenstreet had been partnered by Warner Bros only two years before in *The Maltese Falcon* (1941). They were so successful that the studio repeated the double act, in *Passage to Marseilles* (1944) – and *Casablanca*.

Dooley Wilson was a singer, not a piano player (that was played by an off-screen Elliott Carpenter) – as much as an actor, and was not first choice for the part of Sam. At one point it was possible that Lena Horne would play the part – as 'Samantha', rather than Sam. Wilson's screen test for the role was not brilliant, according to Hal Wallis, but once screenwriter Casey Robinson got to work on the script the character was foregrounded and Wilson found himself in the role of a lifetime.

The major relationships in the film are those between Bogart and Bergman, and Bogart and Rains. Paul Henreid's Laszlo is a frustratingly elusive character, devoid of any real romantic passion, and thus little more than a cipher for both the underground resistance plot, and the featured love story.

Wilson's character was foregrounded

Dooley Wilson as Sam,
playing the role of a lifetime

CLAUDE RAINS

In some ways, the relationship between Captain Renault and Rick can be called the real emotional heart of the film; theirs is the 'beautiful friendship' beginning as the film ends.

Rains's story is an extraordinary one – one is almost tempted to say a 'Hollywood' one. A cockney boy who could not pronounce his 'r's', he became a stage actor in London in his teens and early twenties; George Bernard Shaw called him his 'favourite interpreter'. *Casablanca* was his thirty-second film; by then he was financially secure enough not to feel the need to be under contract.

Rains's strength was in his voice, and his ability to play what have been called 'suave degenerates'. Not burdened by starry looks or persona (at five-foot-five he was considerably shorter than Ingrid Bergman and had to stand on a crate in their scenes together) he was relatively free to act, and his Captain Renault is a memorable creation – far removed from the Bogartian Rick, or the stereotyped Nazi of Conrad Veidt. In fact, Renault became a byword for attractive duplicity and cynicism.

INGRID BERGMAN

Ingrid Bergman was spotted in the Swedish original of the film *Intermezzo* (1936) and immediately lined up for the Hollywood remake, playing opposite Leslie Howard, three years afterwards. She was one of a number of European actresses considered initially for the part of Ilsa – others included Hedy Lamarr, Michelle Morgan, and the Russian ballerina Tamara Toumanova.

In effect, Bergman's career was 'owned' at this stage by David O. Selznick, the independent producer responsible for *Gone With the Wind* (1939), and Warner Bros – in the persons of scriptwriters Phillip and Julius Epstein – had to 'pitch' for her to join the cast.

Bergman the actress was a contrast of steely ambition and openness, almost naïveté. Her persona offered the appeal of virginal grace which made her later affair with Italian film director Roberto Rossellini all the more shocking to movie-going America. Her looks and middle-register voice offered a sexiness that was at odds with her assumed innocence.

cynical persona

Once the American 'Lois' was dropped from the original stageplay, it was apparent that a European – and this European in particular – was exactly the right choice. Curiously, the lack of on-set chemistry between her and Bogart is almost legendary, although she always claimed he treated her with charm and respect. How they combined to portray one of the cinema's great love stories is often cited as the film's central enigma.

HUMPHREY BOGART

Humphrey Bogart came from a solidly middle-class background, the son of a GP and an illustrator. Perhaps the source of his cynical persona lies partly in his disappointment that acting did not constitute a real, 'grown-up' achievement for him. We can almost sense Bogart, the man, in his lines to Laszlo 'We all try ... you succeed'.

Before a couple of false starts in Hollywood in the early 1930s, Bogart had a flourishing acting career on Broadway. Warner's took him up for *The Petrified Forest* in 1936. Once established as a second-row player, he played heavies in his early Warner years – typically being killed before the final reel by Jimmy Cagney or Edward G. Robinson.

The film *High Sierra* (1940) established his 'doomed' persona as a leading man in 1940; and his star potential was spotted about the time he starred in *The Maltese Falcon* (1941). That he should come to stardom relatively late is surprising, except for the fact that his appeal is as an older, wiser, cynical tough guy who has been around the block.

In fact, were it not for the fact that Warner Bros stars Paul Muni and George Raft – the only real competitors for this persona – were on the wane, Bogart might never have been taken up at all. Nevertheless, a decision was taken in 1940–41 to 'build' Bogart as a leading man, and the part of Rick was written from the start with him – and this – in mind.

Bogart was notoriously uncomfortable playing romantic roles, at least before he starred with Lauren Bacall – who became his fourth and final wife, and the one with whom he was finally happy – in *To Have and Have Not* (1945). Perhaps the source of his discomfort was in a series of increasingly disastrous relationships with women. By 1942, he was married to the violently jealous Mayo Methot, and accounts of the making of the film recall numerous on-set feuds, fights, and even a stabbing (see Sperber and Lax, 1997).

Casablanca ended up playing to his strengths: the wise-cracking lines, the half-shadows, and, most of all, the core of moral decency – what Bacall called his 'integrity' – have all become synonymous with his persona, along with the trenchcoat and hat.

authorship

That a film should have an 'author' is in many ways an absurd idea. Film-making is so much a collaborative enterprise that it does not fit our commonsense ideas of how art is made – the lone artist, engaged in creative struggle, bringing a work to life from his (and the stereotype is male) imagination. Although many claims have been made for film-making as an artistic process – and for film itself as '*le septieme art*' in France anyway – it is still primarily a commercial and industrial activity. In the 1930s and 1940s, film-making in Hollywood was perfected as an industrial enterprise – called the studio system.

The claim that films are 'authored' by their directors was established by an influential group of French film directors and critics writing for a film journal in the 1950s, *Cahiers du Cinema*. The original idea was promulgated in a kind of manifesto, the 'politique des auteurs' in the 1950s (see Cook, 1999). The movers behind the 'politique' included Jean Luc Godard, François Truffaut, Claude Chabrol and Andre Bazin, and focused on American directors such as Orson Welles and Nicholas Ray, and the English director Alfred Hitchcock, by then working in Hollywood.

The impetus behind the theory was to recuperate film-making from being a commercially-driven industrial process, in which the director was just one cog in an enormous machine, to an artistic process in which the director's vision was paramount.

Identifying the markers of an auteur in a director's body of work became a pre-occupation, to the extent that even the inferior works of an important director became more important than the most commercially successful mainstream film.

This sense still lingers in the understanding and appreciation of directors today: film critics still anxiously await the latest films by established directors like Martin Scorsese, Tim Burton, Quentin Tarantino in the US, and Mike Leigh and Ken Loach in Britain. However, even the Hollywood marketing machines now incorporate the notion of 'authorship' in their publicity, selling the involvement of someone like Quentin Tarantino in films even where he only has had a tangential role.

The 'politique des auteurs' has been countered, or superseded, by a range of other critical approaches since the 1950s. Films which could not be appropriated to the 'auteur' principles were recognised in the 1960s under genre theory, so Westerns, musicals, gangster films came to be interpreted and respected for other reasons, and the directors of important genre films became admitted to the canon of 'auteurs'.

In the 1970s and 1980s, the role of audiences in creating meaning in films was treated more seriously, particularly in relation to how audiences are prepared for the conventions and pleasures of genre films, and, later, in the creation of stars. Richard Dyer's *Stars*, published in 1979, established the study of stars as a legitimate route to understanding how films work.

THE GENIUS OF THE SYSTEM

In 1989 a book was published which challenged the orthodoxy that authorship was a concept restricted to the individual, often maverick, director, with a unique cinematic style and sensibility. Called *The Genius of the System*, the book set out to identify what it was about the organisation and method of the major Hollywood studios of the 1930s and 1940s which contributed to the creation of so many lasting commercially and critically successful films.

The argument of the book's author, Thomas Schatz, was that the system itself was responsible for the artistic and commercial success of such films as *Rebecca* (1940), *Gone with the Wind* (1939), *Casablanca* (1942), *Meet Me in St. Louis* (1944), and *A Star is Born* (1937). His real contribution was to identify the role of the studio executive producer in the making of studio films – both in their attention to the content of films, and in their management of the talent creating it.

authorship

For the major film studios of the time, making films was the same as any other form of mass production. Mass production itself has been called a 'Fordist' system, after the conveyor belt model of car-making devised by Henry Ford, and the studio system was certainly Fordist.

Essentially the model was this: a script or treatment would be bought by a studio, particularly if it had obvious roles for contract stars, and a team of writers would be asked to develop it into a screenplay. Usually more than one team of writers would be put on a project, working on the same script independently. Specialist writers would be drafted in to write dialogue, or to ensure continuity of plot and action.

Casting would be carried out while the script was being drafted; screen tests would be set up using sections of the script, or scenes especially written. The shoot would then start on a Monday morning, and typically the director, the technical crew, and some of the actors would have only finished working on another film two days before.

A shoot might take eight weeks, with scenes shot out of sequence according to the availability of key players. Post-production, when the film was edited and a musical score added, was supervised by the production executive. The director and the cast and crew would by now be working on another film.

According to the hunch of the producer, extra scenes or lines of dialogue might be added to the film at this stage. A finished version would be screened for senior studio executives, and more changes might be suggested. The film would preview with test audiences, and yet more changes might be made. The film would then be handed over to the marketing arm of the studio, which was typically situated on the east coast of America.

Every Hollywood studio film was made in this way. The process enabled the studio staff to be working all year round on films as they went through different stages of production; it enabled Warners in 1942, the year *Casablanca* was made, to make thirty-three other films. Even this was down on the year before, when they made forty-eight; the impact of the war on production is visible in the fact that in 1934 Warner Bros made sixty-nine films.

Even so, in August 1942, there were six other films being shot on the Warner Bros lot in August, as *Casablanca* was winding up. A contract director such as Michael Curtiz was able to make eighty-seven films for Warner Bros in twenty-six years, and a staggering 160 throughout his career.

It should be clear, then, that the Hollywood director of the 1930s and 1940s did not have more than a functional role in the making of any one film. Their major input was in supervising the shoot – eight weeks out of maybe eight months. The director had no role in the choosing, buying or writing of a script property; invariably they did not see the script until a couple of days before shooting. Once the film was shot, the studio took control of post-production.

So if the director did not control the process, who did? The answer is that the production supervisor, or production executive, was the key player in the studio system. Each studio had their own *éminence grise* – MGM had Irving Thalberg, renowned as the producer with the most refined cinema sensibility in Hollywood (and immortalised as F. Scott Fitzgerald's Last Tycoon, in the novel of that name) until his death in 1937. MGM also had David O. Selznick until 1935 when he left to become an independent producer of prestige films, including *Gone with the Wind* (1939).

Warner Bros's first 'creative' executive producer was Darryl F. Zanuck whose right hand man was Hal B. Wallis. When Zanuck moved to create an independent production company, which within a few years became the major player 20th Century Fox, Wallis was left as the most senior production supervisor; from 1933, his was the most influential voice in the production of Warner Bros films.

In terms of controlling the production process of Warner's films, Wallis had the key role. By 1942, he had become so powerful that he negotiated himself a deal with Jack Warner whereby he was contracted to make four films a year for the studio. He had sole control over these films – he chose the properties, actors, directors, and crew. His first six films – *Now, Voyager, Desperate Journey, Casablanca, Watch on the Rhine, Princess O'Rourke,* and *Air Force* – received eighteen Oscar nominations, and were all box-office successes, an extraordinary testimony to his commercial acumen.

For *Casablanca*, Wallis approved buying the rights to the original play script, *Everybody Comes to Rick's*, supervised the writers, the casting process, appointed the director and the key technical staff, and the composer Max Steiner. He took great care over the detail of the film; he even wrote the famous last line. As evidence of his attention to detail, Aljean Harmetz quotes an extract from four pages of cutting notes that Wallis sent to the film's editor:

> Take out the group of soldiers before the cut of the loading of the refugees into the patrol wagon ... Trim a little on Rains' line, 'And I am prepared to refuse it.' ... Take out two of the last four shots from Ugarte ... Lose the long shot of the waiter bringing the bottle and glasses. Cut to Bergman right on her line, 'Ask the piano player to come over.' ... Take out that long look of Bergman looking around before she says, 'Where is Rick?'
>
> *Harmetz, p. 261*

A closer look at any of these scenes reveals the small but significant differences that each of these changes makes to the drama and pace of the film. Wallis was also respected by his staff for his understanding of narrative drive, character, and emotion. Unusually for a producer he also had a keen sensitivity to the importance of both music and lighting (see Style).

In one sense, then, Wallis can claim to be the most influential of the authors of *Casablanca*, but there are others who have claims, too. In addition to Murray Burnett and his wife Joan Alison, who wrote the original stage play, there were four other writers who had key roles, and each of them put their own stamp on the film. Philip and Julius Epstein, wise-cracking, practical-joking twins, brought a deflating Jewish humour to the romance in a series of crackling one-liners.

However, it was clear to Wallis that the film needed some other authority; it was after all being made just at the time America was entering the Second World War, and Hollywood in general, and Warner Bros in particular, were keen to support the war effort (see Contexts: Hollywood at war). In order that the war in Europe was not just the backdrop for a

authorship background

romantic thriller/melodrama, the politics need to be beefed up. This job was given to Howard Koch, a left-leaning playwright and screenwriter who amongst other things was responsible for *The Sea Hawk* (1940) and *The Letter* (1940), both for Warner Bros. He also wrote the script for the Orson Welles radio play *The War of the Worlds*.

In the later stages of script revision, while the Epsteins and Koch were still, independently, working on it, writer Casey Robinson was drafted in to sharpen the romance. In the original stage-play the relationship between Rick and Ilsa (or Lois, as she was in *Everybody Comes to Rick's*) would not have made it past the Hays Office. Robinson elevated the relationship from a casual sexual liaison to something more noble and tragic. He also strengthened the relationship between Ilsa and Laszlo, so that her loving him, and leaving Rick, had some credibility.

Harmetz credits Robinson with foregrounding the role of Sam. In order to give emotional depth to Ilsa and Rick, he proposed using Sam as a mirror of both of their feelings:

> Scene between Rick and Ilsa is weak. You must heighten here the great fear that Sam has, the almost superstitious darky fear, and also heighten his pleading with Rick to get out of town until this woman is gone.
>
> *Harmetz, p. 176*

What seems to be unusual about Robinson's role is that he is not really a screenwriter as such; rather he edits and analyses extant pieces of script, with a sure sense of how relationships should play, and how to involve the audience. The fact that he did not script specific lines – that, in effect, he was a contract script-doctor – is reflected in his absence from the film's credits.

On their own, it is clear that each of these writers was not capable of producing a script as complex or multi-layered as *Casablanca*. Once production started – and even after it was finished – changes were made. Because these later changes were never formally written down, it is difficult to know who to attribute them to. Legend has it that 'Here's looking at you, kid' was improvised on set by Humphrey Bogart, and Wallis himself wrote the film's final line. The scripting of *Casablanca* thus testifies to the collaborative multi-authored process of film-making typical of the era.

So what, then, was the role of Curtiz? The 'politique des auteurs' stressed that the director – or rather an élite band of directors – authored a film with a personal vision and signature style. The directors favoured by the Cahiers' group included Alfred Hitchcock as the exemplary exponent, and one can see in Hitchcock's films pre-occupations and motifs, even obsessions, recurring with reassuring consistency.

With Curtiz there is no such consistency. Partly this is because, as a contract director for Warners, he made whatever film he was assigned to. Not being a writer, and having no role in pre-production, there was little he could do to influence the conception of any film, and so he did not have the opportunity to stamp on a film his own thematic or generic concerns. He was renowned as a great director of both action and melodrama, and he successfully directed musicals, biopics, and horror films, so he was not given simple genre products to work with.

He was valued for his professional approach, his work rate, his understanding of camera set-ups and shot composition, and these latter two not because he did interesting or innovative things in the frame, like Orson Welles or John Ford, but because he knew exactly how to tell stories visually, with an economy that was in itself elegant. He knew how to pace narratives, so there were no *longeurs* (long drawn out parts) that might pass in other directors for a 'signature visual style'. As he is often quoted, when challenged about continuity, or consistency in character, 'I make them so fast nobody notices'.

Curtiz's emphasis on the visual in his film direction might be accounted for by a number of factors. As a Hungarian émigré, who had made films in Austria, Czechoslovakia, Germany, and Denmark before coming to America in 1926, he was less likely to have a sensitivity to dialogue, especially in English. Indeed, Harmetz points out the role of the dialogue coach in studio films of the 1930s, particularly important with the high proportion of European émigré directors in Hollywood, many of whom had fled Nazi Germany in the 1930s. Also, of course, any director who had learned their trade before 1927 was entirely used to constructing visual narratives, working as they did in the silent era of film-making.

Curtiz's style was thus often misconstrued as being distinctly unfriendly to actors. In fact, this was more to do with his understanding of actors as elements in the composition of the frame than with any diffidence or rudeness on his part. Byron Haskin, quoted in James Robertson's *The Casablanca Man* (1993), called him 'the Busby Berkeley of drama' (p. 140).

Curtiz is difficult to pigeonhole as a director. Among his successes with Warner Bros were *The Adventures of Robin Hood* (1938), *Angels With Dirty Faces* (1938), *Dodge City* (1939), *The Sea Wolf* (1941), *Yankee Doodle Dandy* (1942) and *Mildred Pierce* (1945). His range even here includes a gangster film, a Western, a swashbuckling adventure, a musical biopic, and a melodrama.

Maybe his adeptness with each of these forms led to a critical suspicion that a director who could turn his hand to anything somehow lacked the artistic integrity necessary to be called an 'auteur'. Working with genres was in itself an indicator of a director's lack of artistic independence. A critic such as Andrew Sarris (in Robertson, 1993, p. 2) sees him as too much the compliant studio employee, without a personal artistic vision, to be thought of as an auteur. However, in a telling revelation, he credits *Casablanca* as an exception:

> The director's one enduring masterpiece is, of course, Casablanca, the happiest of happy accidents, and the most decisive exception to the auteur theory.
>
> *Robertson, p. 2*

One could take this further; the fact that Curtiz does not conform to the profile of the film 'auteur' might single him out – rather than just *Casablanca* – as a decisive exception to the auteur theory. His importance lies in the scope of his body of work – over 160 films – rather than in any single film. (For a fuller account of critical debates over the auteur status of Curtiz, see Robertson, 1993, pp. 2–3.)

It is not really possible – or desirable – to come to any definite conclusions about the paramount 'authoring' role of any single member of the team

Bogart and Bergman,
portraying one of cinema's
great love stories

who made *Casablanca*. Indeed, there are key personnel, not even mentioned here, who made invaluable contributions to the outcome. Max Steiner turned 'As Time Goes By' into one of the most potent signature tunes of perhaps any film, even though he did not actually write the song. Arthur Edeson, the film's cinematographer, did a great deal to create the characters of Rick and Ilsa – and the personas of Bogart and Bergman – through his meticulous lighting set-ups. And, of course, Bogart and Bergman themselves manufactured in their performances one of the most passionate cinematic love stories.

The likelihood is that a particularly fertile circumstance – Warner Bros in 1942 – produced what Sarris called 'the happiest of happy accidents'.

narrative & form

Stories are one of the major modes through which society talks to itself, and makes sense of itself; in this century, films are perhaps the dominant mode of storytelling in Western culture.

The study of the structure of stories has been formalised into a quasi-science – narratology; the object of study, the structures studied, have been called narrative. We will now consider some of the features of narrative form.

plot & story

E.M. Forster came up with the still workable distinction between plot and story. The sentence 'the king died and then the queen died', he said, is a story; 'the king died and then the queen died of grief', on the other hand, is a plot. A plot, therefore, is a sequence of events that are linked by cause and effect.

Forster was working with definitions arrived at coincidentally by a group of Russian Formalist critics, for whom narrative was a key area of interest. They, too, distinguished between the story (*fabula*) and the plot (*sjuzet*). For them (see Chatman, 1978) the story is the total sequence of events represented or referred to in a narrative, while the plot is the peculiar ordering of those events. This distinction is referred to elsewhere as that between 'story' and 'discourse'.

Thus, the story events in *Casablanca* include the flashback scenes in Paris, the possibility that Rick and Ilsa spend the night together when she visits him above the bar, and Rick's journey to Brazzaville with Captain Renault. If the story events referred to in the film were arranged in chronological order, one would probably start with Ilsa having a brace fitted to her teeth in 1930 (from the flashback scene 'What were you doing, say, ten years ago?' Rick's answer to the same question, 'Looking for a job', probably does not constitute a story *event*).

Filming the
Paris café scenes

Those three story events – the flashback scene, the night which they may have spent together, and the 'beautiful friendship' are all placed in a plot structure. First of all, the flashback. The Paris scenes of the film were the first to be filmed, on 25 May 1942, and yet they come into the film proper at about a third of the way in, after Ilsa and Laszlo have arrived at Rick's café. We have already seen Sam's recognition of Ilsa, and followed his cue that she represents trouble for Rick. The flashback comes after this as an explanation of this enigma, and a deepening of both Rick and Ilsa's character; it introduces the love story.

The flashback is, thus, a feature of plot structure that either explains/ solves an enigma (common in detective films), or which deepens a relationship. Some films are narrated entirely in flashback, like *Double Indemnity* (1944), or *Mildred Pierce* (1945). In the former, the effect is to set up a kind of inevitability in the fate of the two central characters, as the film is narrated by the dying protagonist.

The second story event picked out from *Casablanca* is the night when Ilsa comes to see Rick. Much has been made of whether this scene constitutes a night of passion for the two characters. The convention of the dissolve used at the end of the scene is that it is the equivalent of drawing a discrete veil over what happened next. More conventionally, of course, it just signifies the passage of time.

At a time of great sensitivity to the strictures of the Hays Office, and the Motion Picture Production Code (or Hays Code), and when the first reader of the playscript *Everybody Comes to Rick's* felt that much of the material was censorable, it may have been a way of safely introducing a riskier eroticism to the film and the central relationship.

These three story events from the film exemplify two of the three features or categories of narrative structure – order, duration, and frequency. The story events in a plot can be presented in a wide range of orders, from flashback to flash forward. Directors such as Quentin Tarantino have rewritten the rule book on narrative order. In films like *Pulp Fiction* (1994), the ordering of story events becomes so complex as to destabilise any notional relationship between plots and reality.

time & narrative

Duration is the second key category of narrative presentation. Ellipsis, as in the example cited from *Casablanca*, is when a story event is left out, or implied. This may be because leaving out story events creates an enigma in the narrative, and a desire to know in the audience, or because it is redundant story information. In *Psycho*, Marion Crane's car journey takes a day and a night, but we are only shown a few minutes of it. The scene of her waking in the car shows us that she has been travelling overnight.

Also in *Psycho* (1960), the crucial piece of narrative information that Norman's mother is dead is withheld from us; this does not create an enigma narrative, but instead shocks and surprises when the information is finally given to us – in the form of her dressed skeleton in the rocking chair.

Besides ellipsis, the other aspects of duration are summary, stretch, pause, and scene. Respectively, these refer to other possible relationships between diegetic or 'film' time, and 'real' time – the time experience of the audience while they are watching the film.

A 'stretch' is when the time taken to complete an action in the film seems longer than it should be, either through slow-motion, or through an extended set of edits. The famous Odessa Steps sequence of *Battleship Potemkin* (1925) is an example of film time stretched by this method; the shots of pram, steps, woman, soldiers, elongate the time we think the pram should take to fall down the steps.

A 'pause' is when the diegetic/film time stops for a moment; the most typical example is in voice-over when film events are related to us, rather than shown to us.

The opening credits of a film can also be an example of a pause, if no direct action from the film is shown, but we are shown something from the world we are about to enter. An example of this kind of pause comes in the opening credits to *The English Patient* (1996), where an unseen hand paints an image of a man falling from the sky. These are elements related to the world of the film – we see images like this in the cave paintings – but it bears no relation to diegetic time, as it is not placed in the film world. Similarly the opening voice-over of *Casablanca* is a kind of pause – place and general time are established, but we are not introduced to the 'film time' of the characters.

'Scene' is when diegetic time and real time overlap completely. Dialogue sequences in films are the most common example of 'scenes'; one of the features of dialogue is that it has to be played out in real time. Extended sequences of dialogue are relatively rare in mainstream film; an interesting example of an extended 'scene', where dialogue between a number of characters is played out, comes in Ken Loach's film *Land and Freedom* (1995) during the scene where a group of villagers argue about collectivisation.

Finally, 'summary' is where a chunk of film time is reduced to a short series of shots, or montage sequence. The clichéd example of a summary might be the use of a montage of newspaper front pages to signify key story events. In *Casablanca* the driving scenes in the Paris flashback sequence effect a kind of summary: they signify a generalised period of pleasure and enjoyment for Rick and Ilsa. Summaries like this were important but not crucial sequences of a film and were managed by lower-status film-making personnel. The montage editor in *Casablanca* was Don Siegel, who later became the director of *The Killers* (1964) and the first of Clint Eastwood's Dirty Harry films.

NARRATIVE RANGE AND DEPTH

Another way of examining narrative form is to think of events as items of information. In this sense, we can talk about both the range and depth of narrative information. Under range, there is a continuum from broad to narrow, where broad can cover narrative events spanning continents and centuries, and narrow can focus on the lives of one or two characters during real time, that is the two hours or so it takes to play out the film.

In terms of narrative range, one can, therefore, contrast a film such as *Birth of a Nation* (1915), (or *Bill and Ted's Excellent Adventure*, 1988 if you want an example of broad narrative range parodied), with some of the real-time films of Andy Warhol such as *Kitchen* (1966), and *Empire* (1962).

range and depth of narration

'Depth' of narrative information ranges on a continuum from objective to subjective. Again, *Birth of a Nation* can serve as an example of objective narration, as the film does not follow the lives or life of single protagonists. At the other end of the scale is a film such as *Taxi Driver* (1976), which is narrated/projected almost entirely from the subjective experience of its central character, Travis Bickle.

Subjective narration has different layers: on the one hand 'perceptual subjectivity' refers to the parts of a film where we see or hear exactly what one character does, as in the opening sequence of *Halloween* (1978); 'mental subjectivity' refers to deeper, more impressionistic rendering of the experience of a character's consciousness, and again Travis Bickle serves as the example here.

In terms of *Casablanca*, the range and depth of narration varies subtly throughout the film. The opening montage and voice-over is relatively objective, and the range of narration narrows from a picture of war-torn Europe, to Casablanca, to the first shot inside Rick's café, where the majority of the film will be set. In terms of depth, the narrative alternates between our view of Rick as it were from the outside, as he is seen by others, to sometimes quite intimate access to his feelings. The Paris flashback scenes are overlain with the pain of his memories, felt through a drunken haze, and are thus quite subjective.

These are general observations about narrative in *Casablanca*, rather than a detailed analysis of its structure, scene by scene. Before progressing to that, some explanation of various models of narrative is necessary.

narrative models & their uses

The models of narrative most often applied in relation to film are those developed by Propp, Todorov, and David Bordwell. In addition there are understandings of narrative based on structuralist principles, and the anthropology of Levi-Strauss.

Propp

In Propp's 'Morphology of the Russian Folk Tale' (1975), Propp proposed two radical ideas about narrative. The first was that characters are just as much narrative functions as they are representations of people; that is, they have roles in discharging and progressing the narrative of a text.

Second, he proposed that the events in a narrative could be reduced to a kind of general template, and that all narratives choose events from this repertoire of thirty-one generalised events, and present them in roughly the same order.

He claimed to identify only eight broad character types in the thousands of folk tales he analysed:

- the villain
- the donor
- the helper
- the princess
- the despatcher
- the hero or victim
- the false hero

To reinforce this sense of character not as person but as narrative function, he renamed character as a 'sphere of action'. Thus, he was able to claim that not every narrative would contain these eight – and only these eight – character functions: some of the roles would be carried out by the same person, so, for example, the false hero and the villain could be played by the same person, as could the donor and the despatcher.

Much has been made of the 'fit' between Propp's character functions and a range of canonical Hollywood films; Graeme Turner, (1988), for example, matches them against *Star Wars* (1977) quite easily. A cursory application of Propp's model of functions to *Casablanca* will reveal both its strengths and its weaknesses.

The villain of the film is, in one sense, straightforwardly Major Strasser; he stands for Nazi Germany, to which the refugee community of Casablanca – and by implication, the audience, and the Allies – is opposed. At times,

overlapping of functions

the ambivalent French prefect of police, Captain Renault, also carries a proportion of the villain role.

The hero function is, also straightforwardly, taken by Rick, although the resistance leader Laszlo shares it, too, and in the resolution of the film Renault's allegiance switches so that he too becomes a hero. In this sense, this sharing of functions is allowed for by Propp, as one character can move between functions, and a single character function can be shared between characters. What the model does not explain is the process by which these roles are shared, and how the narrative plays them out.

The princess function is uncomplicatedly taken on by Ilsa; she is the 'object' lost and, briefly, sought by Rick, even though at the end maybe Renault has become Rick's princess. (It is worth remembering that the relationship between Rick and Renault has been called the true love story at the heart of the film.)

The functions of donor, helper, despatcher can be matched with, respectively, Ugarte, Renault, and Rick himself, but it is difficult to find a character to match the 'false hero' function. In some ways Renault should be a hero – he is a functionary in a free French state. The fact that he cosies up to Strasser, and does not go out of his way to help Rick or Laszlo until the very end, might qualify him as false hero – but equally he could be called false villain. Rick, too, in the sense that he is, at his lowest point, his own worst enemy – and representative of isolationist America – could be called a false hero.

In the end, though, the overlapping of functions is so widespread that Propp's typology becomes close to useless; what we are left with is an ensemble of complex characters who cannot be reduced to single functions, and who change and develop throughout the film. Thus, the major problem with Propp's character types is that often film characters have more pleasures to offer the audience than the simple discharging of plot. The processes of identification that we go through depend on cleverly-drawn characters, who offer us value added over and above their narrative role.

Propp and Vogler

Propp's other contribution to narrative theory – his thirty-one 'actions' or narrative stages – have been transformed by the Hollywood treatment-writer and script-reader, Christopher Vogler, into a template or narrative recipe for the successful Hollywood film (Vogler, 1996). Propp's model is dealt with in some detail elsewhere (Turner, 1988). This next section looks a little more closely at Vogler's model.

Vogler was a story analyst, employed specifically to research narratives from all over the world, and detailed to come up with story ideas. Following his reading of Joseph Campbell's *The Hero with a Thousand Faces*, he began to devise a master narrative template which he claimed the majority of Hollywood films had in common.

His model describes twelve stages in a film plot:

- Ordinary world
- Call to adventure
- Refusal of the call
- Meeting the mentor
- Crossing the first threshold
- Tests, allies, enemies
- Approach to the inmost cave
- Supreme ordeal
- Reward (seizing the sword)
- Road back
- Resurrection
- Return with elixir

When applied to popular fairy-tale-like plots such as those of *Pretty Woman* (1990), *Star Wars* (1977), and *The Wizard of Oz* (1939), Vogler's model seems to work. How applicable is it to *Casablanca*?

The ordinariness of *Casablanca*'s 'Ordinary World' lies in the constant unpredictability that its inhabitants are subject to. The line of dialogue 'round up the usual suspects' refers to an almost cynical approach to law and order. Rick's ordinary world – his routines – are quickly established in a series of decisions he makes in the opening: allowing credit from some guests, refusing others.

The Call to Adventure – and its partial refusal – are represented by Ugarte's presentation of the letters of transit. He is invited to participate in some nefarious dealings, something which is out of the ordinary for Rick, but agrees only to hold the letters until the evening.

So far, straightforward. It is only when considering the nature of the hero's journey that things become complicated. The letters of transit turn out after all to be only a plot device: they are not of central concern to Rick. His twin drives from here on, are in recapturing the affections of Ilsa, and in securing a safe passage for Ilsa and Laszlo. The two drives are incompatible, and the moment when he chooses one above the other – after Ilsa visits him for the second time – is his Supreme Ordeal.

What makes the narrative of *Casablanca* more complex than Vogler's simple model is the fact that Rick's journey, goals, and drives are all interiorised; it is not a matter of stealing an emerald, as in *Romancing the Stone* (1984) or of destroying the Deathstar and winning the princess, as in *Star Wars* (1977). Instead, the film follows a struggle of conscience, a transformation in a code of behaviour, in which the ostensible plot, centring on the theft of important letters, is really only a cipher, a surface device on which to structure a deeper set of movements.

Rick's reward is not so much self-knowledge, as the recovery of the person he was in Paris. He has been through an almost therapeutic journey, where a psychic obstacle – his rejection by Ilsa – is removed by a process of reflection and new information. When he overcomes this obstacle he is able to behave 'correctly' and return to his older 'normal' self.

STRUCTURALISM

An alternative approach to narrative study, and one which seems to offer a more fruitful understanding of *Casablanca*, comes from the structuralist tradition of literary and cultural criticism. Initially coming from an analysis of the structure of language, structuralism came to be applied to the analysis of a whole range of cultural phenomena. Its chief populariser,

Roland Barthes, famously applied the method to wrestling, advertising and Greta Garbo's photograph, in his short book *Mythologies* (1989).

The power of *Mythologies* is that it uses the structuralist method to explain the role of myth as one of societies' chief methods of representing its conflicts and tensions. Barthes said that myth resolves incompatible sets of oppositions for us in ways that are not possible in the real world. They are a kind of social wish fulfilment.

Contemporary myths for Barthes were reproduced by the cinema. Many film critics and academics have picked up his notion of myth – and that of Levi-Strauss – and applied it to the study of genres, stars, and individual films.

The structuralist method rests on the positing of a set of oppositions within the object of study. These binary structures are either thought to be somehow hard-wired in human consciousness, or common to a diverse range of human societies and cultures. Their origin or cause is less interesting – or determinable – than the way they are manifested in particular texts or products.

The Western genre, for example, has been analysed in terms of its resolution of these sets of opposites (see Nelmes, 1999), which run something like this:

■ civilisation   wilderness
■ indoors   outdoors
■ female   male
■ the law   natural justice
■ community   individual

Only the hero of the Western is able to move across these oppositions, unifying or resolving them. Thus, a series of intractable tensions that threaten social order are made better or more palatable by the action of a lonely gun-slinger.

The binary structure, typical of this approach to film, can be applied to *Casablanca*. Indeed the film critic Robert B. Ray has suggested that *Casablanca* follows some of the formal properties of the Western (1985).

Like the Western, a lone male, with a shady past, is called upon to save civilisation and its values by transgressing the law. The punishment for the hero is that, having broken the law in the pursuit of justice, and while saving the day, he is not able to live in that civilised society. His strength and power come from his outsider status, and he has to return to the wilderness from whence he came. This pattern is replayed in countless canonical Westerns, from *Stagecoach* (1939), to *The Searchers* (1956), to *Shane* (1953), and *Unforgiven* (1991). It is also the structure of *Casablanca*.

In typical Westerns, the hero develops an attachment for a woman who represents the civilised and civilising values associated with femininity. Because of his outsider status, however, the hero cannot consummate this relationship, and returns to the wilderness alone. Exceptions to this model of male-female relations include *Stagecoach*, where John Wayne goes into the wilderness with Claire Trevor, the reformed prostitute and fellow outsider. In a parallel to this, Rick and Renault ride off together into the sunset.

CLASSICAL HOLLYWOOD NARRATIVE

The final model to be looked at in conjunction with the film is David Bordwell's classical Hollywood narrative. Bordwell (1985) watched and analysed Hollywood films made between 1920 and 1960, and deduced from these a set of principles by which he claimed the Hollywood film of this period operated.

First of all, the narrative follows the desire(s) of a single protagonist. He (invariably he) is seeking something – revenge or restitution, love, the solution to a crime, buried treasure; the source of narrative tension lies in the range of obstacles put in the protagonist's way. Very few mainstream films of this period do not follow the trajectory of a single character, though it is more common in non-mainstream films, and is becoming more common in contemporary mainstream cinema.

Second, the narrative follows a series of events linked in time and place by cause and effect. Coherence of time and place is maintained by this cause-and-effect structure. Events that have no place in a cause-and-effect chain are rare in classic Hollywood cinema, and indeed we are almost trained to watch films like this. Scenes in a film which have no immediate place in the cause-effect structure alert us to their probable significance later on.

Thirdly, mainstream narratives follow a consistent pattern, from the disruption of a kind of stasis, stability, or equilibrium at the opening of the film, to a gradual return to stasis or equilibrium by its close. Open-ended endings were rare in Hollywood until production companies cottoned on to the potential of making sequels to popular films.

The articulation of these elements depended on the genre of the film: thus the opening of a Western might feature the disruption of a small community gathered together for a social event, like a wedding or a dinner, by a band of outlaws. A second immediate disruption might be the arrival of a mysterious lone gun-slinger. The narrative may then follow the attempt of both lone hero and community to restore social order, which invariably happens. This is the model followed by *Shane*, for example.

PLOTTING CASABLANCA

The match between this 1987 model and *Casablanca*, which was made in the middle of the period of cinema which Bordwell studied to arrive at his schema, is quite interesting.

Act one

The initial disruption, the announcement of the theft of the letters of transit, and the rounding up of the usual suspects culminating in the death of one of them, signals in some ways that disruption is the normal mode of events in Casablanca. There is no settled pattern of social behaviour here; rather, as the portentous voice-over announces, Casablanca is a kind of limbo where everyone is waiting, waiting, waiting.

Rick, however, who we are introduced to after eight minutes, is one of the few characters who does not seem to be waiting. In the opening half-hour, his character is established as ostensibly neutral, but latently antipathetic to the Nazis; casual with women; and scrupulously protective of his staff. His solid isolationist stance is not disrupted until the arrival of Ilsa and Laszlo. As Renault points out, a number of precedents are set here: for the first time he drinks with guests, and picks up the tab, and also for the first time, Sam plays 'As Time Goes By'.

The music itself heralds the disruption of Rick's cosy self-reliance. Sam warns Ilsa he should not play it – which signals to us something of an enigmatic past on Rick's behalf.

So, this is equilibrium disrupted on a number of different levels – first in the superficial narrative, and second in the behaviour and demeanour of the major character. In addition to this, there is the arrival of Major Strasser, himself a bird of ill omen for this Free French colony, and the announcement by Renault of the impending arrest of the thief of the letters of transit.

Each of these maintains the pace of the narrative; different hares are started, and one, the arrest of Ugarte, is concluded. All this happens in the first thirty-two minutes – effectively the first Act of this three-act drama.

Act two

This begins with Rick drinking alone in the darkened bar. The fade to black of the previous shot – a pensive Captain Renault watching the exit of Laszlo and Ilsa – signals to us a passage of time – an ellipsis. The sight of Rick drunk, suddenly, without warning, reinforces the disruption to his own equanimity; the fact that he does not drink with customers leads us to see him as a man in control, restrained, aloof, and yet here he is completely undone. We have also only seen him so far in the company of others; now, but for Sam in the darkness behind him, he is alone, to all intents and purposes, and emotionally quite vulnerable.

Up to now we have only been given a relatively objective narrative point of view. The camera has ranged freely across a range of characters; Rick has come in and out of focus, but it is clear that we are being involved in the drama of a community, and of the politics that will shape their destiny. With the scene in the empty bar, we enter a more private world. Also, we enter a more subjective narrative viewpoint. The flashback to the Paris scenes starts here, with Rick's maudlin self-pity; this section of narrative information is known only to him and Sam – it has become interiorised.

The purpose of the flashback is two-fold. An enigma has been set up in the narrative: the urbane, cool, cynical bar owner, who cheeks the Nazis, who sticks his neck out for no-one, has been destabilised by the arrival of a beautiful woman in his bar. That she is with her husband makes the situation complicated. Some explanation is necessary; what is there between Rick and Ilsa? Why aren't they together now?

The flashback scenes give us some satisfaction – they signal a brighter, more optimistic time, when Rick was less cynical, more open, and was called 'Richard'. They make clear that something went wrong the day the Germans entered Paris. They, in fact, set up a further enigma: why didn't Ilsa meet Rick on the station platform, and how did she come to be with Laszlo?

When we return to Rick's stupor, upstairs in his office, Ilsa comes to him. We are promised a resolution of her enigmatic non-appearance at the train station in Paris, but Rick blows it by being rude and aggressive. She withholds this crucial piece of information from him – and from us.

At this point, it is not clear what it is that Rick wants, in narrative terms. In one sense, his desire has been to repress any memory of Ilsa and Paris; this is where the cynical exterior comes from. He is by now the unwilling bearer of the letters of transit, but he is inert in using or profiting from them. When Ilsa returns to him, she not only plants a desire for an explanation in us, but also in Rick. This is the first time in the film that Rick wants something, but for the moment he will have to wait.

The next scene, in Renault's office, has been carefully set up during Laszlo's encounter with Strasser the evening before. Laszlo and Ilsa are refused a visa by Renault, and they are given the news that Ugarte is dead, so no letters of transit. Some of the burden of whose desires the narrative follows is now shouldered by them; they are becoming desperate to leave Casablanca as what they thought was a relatively straightforward flight has become strewn with obstacles. This will lead them to Rick – just at the moment when he wants something from them.

The scene in the bazaar between Ilsa and Rick is in many ways pivotal. Laszlo goes to see Ferrari about buying visas; Ilsa bumps into Rick while listlessly looking at lace. Robert McKee has done a bravura exegesis of this short scene between the two leads (in a special edition of the BBC2 arts programme *The Late Show*). He breaks down the sequence into a series of 'beats' or interactions or moves in the conversation. At each turn Rick is either aggressive or aggrieved. He wants not only an explanation, but also possibly a signal that their affair might be rekindled. He finally pushes her too far, and she admits that she is married to Laszlo.

Throughout the scene, Rick is positioned on the left hand side of the frame, with Ilsa on the right. McKee points out that the left side of a frame is traditionally seen as being an insecure position, while the right is much more stable. Rick has thus become almost completely unravelled, from the position of seeming invulnerability at the start. He has been forced to relive a powerful affair, has been given the explanation that he wanted, and now is desolate. Ironically, Ilsa and Laszlo are just about to be sent – by Ferrari – back to Rick as their only hope of escaping from Casablanca.

After this brief moment of desire on Rick's part, the narrative follows the desires of other characters. He helps out the Bulgarian couple – either as a 'gesture to love', as he drily remarks to Renault, or out of a spiteful, or chivalrous desire to spike Renault's philandering with the young girl. The motives are clearly mixed, but he is cast as 'helper' here. The narrative ranges across the café again; an elderly German couple are practising their English; Curt Bois's pickpocket is prowling; Yvonne is consorting with the enemy. When the young Annina poses her hypothetical question to Rick, the depth of his disillusionment is clear: 'Nobody ever loved me that much'.

When Rick refuses Laszlo's request for the letters of transit – even when he backs it up with a speech about saving the free world – we are at a narrative impasse, and something has to break the log-jam. That something is the famous musical duelling scene.

In many ways, *Casablanca*, like many Hollywood films of the time, is dialogue-heavy. The plot centres on intrigue and relationships: much of the narrative information is conveyed in talk between characters. But some key meanings/effects/movements happen outside language, as if language itself reaches a dead-end.

The singing of the 'Marseillaise' effectively breaks the deadlock at this point. Laszlo cannot persuade Rick to part with the letters using his considerable rhetoric. Instead, quite by chance, he is given the opportunity to persuade by other means. The singing of the ultra-patriotic French national anthem is what effects a change in Rick's sympathies. The band look to him when Laszlo asks them to play it, and he nods his assent.

narrtative models

The playing of
the 'Marseillaise':
pivotal narrative moment
in *Casablanca*

It is important to note throughout these scenes how the film moves between the personal interactions of Rick with Laszlo and Ilsa, and the more generalised action, the comings and goings in the bar. It is as if narrative structure has to be carefully plotted so that there are alternations between the moments of high drama – or melodrama – and the context in which the drama is set.

Roland Barthes (in Chatman, 1978) referred to two orders of narrative event: the kernel and the satellite. Just as they sound, the former refers to central events or moments in the cause-effect structure of a plot, while the latter refers to those peripheral events which, while not central, are still necessary as they give the major moments room to build up and amplify.

A sophisticated plotter, such as the combined writers of *Casablanca*, will maintain connections between satellite and kernel narrative moments, and will occasionally spring surprises on us: the 'Marseillaise' sequence is one such. What starts out as a competition between two opposing groups of patriots comes to be seen as a turning point in the demeanour of the major character.

The other result of the singing of the 'Marseillaise' is, of course, that the bar is closed. This provides the opportunity to remove the colourful émigré nightlife as a distraction from what is about to become the main business of the feature: resolving the love triangle and hatching the escape plan.

Act three

This starts after this impasse has been breached: Rick is ready to make a decision – we don't know which way he will swing, and he is not going to make up his mind immediately, but dramatically the seeds of resolution have been sown.

In the scene in Laszlo's hotel room, Ilsa and Victor come to an understanding. It is clear to him that she has had some kind of affair with Rick, and that it is she who must get the letters of transit for their escape. In an implicit parallel with Jan and Annina's story, they silently assent to her sleeping with Rick in return for the letters.

At Rick's, Ilsa has second guessed both him and us: she is waiting for him when he comes upstairs. The dramatic climax of the film is when Ilsa pulls a gun on Rick – and then capitulates to him. This is where the famous dissolve happens, and it must signify some censorable activity: the following scene has her telling him about how she met Laszlo, and finally explaining her absence on the platform of the Paris train station.

Ordinarily, there would be no need for any time to pass between this and their embrace. Here, at last, Rick's actions, rather than his inaction, dominate and drive the narrative. Ilsa says 'You have to do the thinking for both of us, now, for all of us.' Her correction is interesting – was it a Freudian slip? Was the 'both' she and Laszlo, or she and Rick?

From here, the plot is simply a matter of working out the mechanics of the resolution. As Harmetz has pointed out, there was never any doubt about the ending, no matter how many versions were mooted, or even shot. The ending of the film is exactly as it is in the play, and dramatically and in terms of character, and politics (remember this is a propaganda film), Rick has to be separated from Ilsa and she and her freedom fighter have to live to fight another day. Rick, too, like the lone gun-slinger of the Western, has to 'light out' for the wilderness.

A kind of stasis, or equilibrium, is returned to at the end. There is a symmetrical balance in the relationships between Renault and Rick, and between Laszlo and Ilsa; the immediate threat of Major Strasser has been removed; the freedom fighter and his beautiful wife have moved on. The extent to which the narrative has fulfilled or followed any of these people's desires is variable. Only Laszlo really has achieved what he set out to; Ilsa has lost what she belatedly realised she wanted; and Rick has gained what he never consciously sought.

In short, it is much closer to the compromises, dissatisfactions, and partial victories of real life, than to any theoretical narrative model. But then that is how it should be.

style

In the last section, we considered the form, that is the narrative shape, of *Casablanca*. In the study of film, however, the term 'style' is used to describe the cinematic content: the lighting, editing, sound, camera work, and the mise-en-scène. This section continues with a description of each of the elements of film style in relation to *Casablanca*.

mise-en-scène

This widely-used French phrase – literally translated as 'what is put in the scene' – is one of the two core ways of addressing the meaning of a film, the other being editing. Traditionally included under mise-en-scène are six components: the 'technical codes' of lighting, camera work, composition, and the 'cultural codes' of setting, dress, and performance.

The 'technical codes' are techniques which relate specially to film. The 'cultural codes' – which also incorporate dialogue and props – cover conventions which are used in other media, such as the theatre, photography and literature.

Mise-en-scène is more than just an analytical category, however; it can in itself be a whole *aesthetic* in cinema, that is a philosophy of artistic intent.

The film critic Andre Bazin (see Cook, 1999 or 1994) cited mise-en-scène – effectively the *shot* – as being the most important unit of meaning in cinema. This would not be controversial, were it not for the fact that the influential Russian film-maker Eisenstein had previously argued that editing, or montage, was the dominant system of meaning-making in cinema. After all, editing is the one process that is peculiar to film-making.

Bazin, instead, suggested that using the shot, and what is put in it, is the purest form of cinema, the least compromised, the closest to 'reality'. Editing he saw as a kind of impure manipulation of cinematic elements. Film-makers contemporary with Bazin, particularly Robert Bresson in France, exemplified his approach, his aesthetic.

In films such as *Mouchette* (1966) and *Au Hasard Balthazar* (1966), Bresson tells stories in austere pictorial ways, wringing out maximum subtlety and nuance from gesture and facial expression. His camera lingers over shots for what a contemporary audience would think is an inordinate length of time, but the effect is complex, sometimes making the audience identify with character and feelings, sometimes giving the effect of a pitilessly objective observing intelligence. Whatever, the effect is of a film-maker in no hurry to move us or manipulate us.

In one sense, though, the mise-en-scène aesthetic is atypical of mainstream cinema, of which *Casablanca* is a prime example. The driving principle behind the mobilisation of film language in mainstream Hollywood cinema is that *story* should be foregrounded – and in such a way that the audience doesn't notice how it is being constructed. As far as possible, then, the mise-en-scène – and the editing – of classical Hollywood cinema strives to be 'invisible' and 'natural'. This rendering of film construction as invisible has been identified as the 'realist' mode; Bordwell's description of the classic system of Hollywood narrative (see Narrative) comes under the 'realist' rubric. Any description of the style of Casablanca should be made within an understanding of it as a 'realist' film text.

FRAMING, COMPOSITION, CHOREOGRAPHY

Three of the key components of mise-en-scène are framing, composition, and choreography and director Michael Curtiz paid considerable attention to framing and composition, but making them subservient to the story. Any close look at scenes from *Casablanca* will reveal how these elements have been 'naturalised'.

There are three types of set-up in the film: for action, 'colour' (that is social detail), and drama. Each operates according to slightly different priorities, but within 'realist' parameters, that is, centring a single action for us in the frame at any one time; holding the shot for as long as it takes the action to be completed and no longer; cutting to reactions to action as a way of facilitating audience involvement; and holding the camera at a distance from the action so that we 'see everything'. For an indication of how this

mise-en-scène

mode has become conventionalised, compare the mise-en-scène in a studio period Hollywood film with a current American TV drama like *ER, NYPD Blue,* or *Homicide: Life on the Street.* In contemporary drama the filming and framing seem much less staged, more haphazard. What counts as a 'realistic' rendering of action has changed dramatically in the last fifty – maybe even the last ten – years.

The action scenes in *Casablanca* are relatively rare: the rounding up of suspects at the start, the arrest of Ugarte, the shooting of Major Strasser. Michael Curtiz was renowned as a director of action: his previous credits included *Captain Blood* (1935), and *The Adventures of Robin Hood* (1938), both of which starred – and made – Errol Flynn as a swashbuckling adventurer.

Curtiz knew how to film action scenes unobtrusively and economically, with a fixed camera, rapid editing, and the skilful choreography of groups of people. The action scenes are finely paced with insert shots of reactions which manage the suspense – like the pause-shot where Ugarte goes to collect his chips, or the unfortunate suspect at the beginning pretending to fumble for his papers. The camera modulates between medium shots of people making decisions, and long shots of actual events. These sequences end up being effective in an almost seamless way.

The second category of mise-en-scène in the film is those set-ups which establish social background, milieu, and context. Examples include the pickpocket scene with Curt Bois at the beginning, the café scenes – both those where Sam is rousing the patrons, and the finer grained vignettes of émigrés each pursuing their own dreams. One *trope* or visual motif in the film revolves around the immobility of those people stuck in Casablanca. The English couple at the start, the German couple learning English, the gamblers glued to the roulette table – are all not only stuck in Casablanca, they are also immobile in the frame.

Those who can move – like the pickpocket, or Carl the waiter, or Captain Renault and Rick – have a privileged status in the film. The pickpocket, by virtue of his lack of scruple, 'knows the ropes': he weaves in and out of the English couple as though they were beached whales. In a different way Rick and Renault come and go as they please. We see them in the café, in the prefect's offices, at the airport, and in Rick's case, in the bazaar. The fact of their reluctance to leave – or of their resignation to staying in Casablanca – ironically gives them license to rove around the city.

The third type of set-up is those shots which serve to foreground dramatic tension. These shots invariably focus on the two principals – Bogart and Bergman – and not coincidentally, as the studio was keen to give the two actors, especially Bogart, plenty of screen time in order to build and capitalise on their personas. Looking at star figures has been identified as one of the key pleasures of going to the cinema (see Dyer, 1979); we like to admire and identify with beautiful glamorised people, and Bogart and Bergman have two of the most enduring screen presences in cinema.

The drama of these scenes tends to be ratcheted up by the use of close-up photography. Bergman was filmed with net filters over the lens, to reinforce the aura of almost other-worldly beauty. She literally glows in the film, is invariably dressed in white, and projects a strong sense of yearning, optimism and innocence in those shots where her head is tilted upwards looking either into the past or the future, or into Bogart's face.

Bogart, on the other hand, isn't framed by idealising camera work. Instead he is lit ambiguously, sometimes half in shadow, with the brim of his fedora shadowing the top half of his face. *Casablanca* (along with *The Maltese Falcon*, 1941) established the favoured mode for filming Bogart, as a man literally dwelling in shadows, who knows the dark side of life, for whom there is no reason to be optimistic, but likewise no reason to give up, yet.

He is introduced to us enigmatically, in the famous shot of his hand signing his abbreviated name: 'OK, Rick'. Then the camera cuts to show us his chess game (playing against himself, or an absent opponent? Struggling against his own demons?), then finally we see his face. Similarly, in the drunk scene, in the empty bar, late at night, when everyone but Sam has gone home, he is sunk in shadow, only part of his face visible.

Iconically, Ilsa, the angel glowing with hope and 'knowledge, thoughts, and ideals', and Bogart, the cynical wisecracker who resists the limelight, would never be able to get it together. Ilsa belongs with the other idealist, idealised, white-suited European, Laszlo.

placement of characters

The tension existing between Bogart and Bergman is beautifully handled in Curtiz's mise-en-scène. Earlier, in Narrative and Form (Plotting *Casablanca*), the scene between them in the bazaar is looked at closely, and you will remember there how important the placement of characters is in the frame.

The position of characters relative to each other in a shot can express as much about their relationship as does their language. Often, it can work in counterpoint to what the characters are saying. Robert Ray (1985) looks in detail at another sequence of the film, when Rick joins Ilsa, Laszlo, and Renault at their table. At this point in the film Laszlo and Renault know nothing of Rick and Ilsa's history; we have had only an inkling from Ilsa's recognition of Sam, his troubled look on her arrival, and Rick's truncated admonition to Sam not to play 'As Time Goes By'.

In the sequence at the table, as Ray points out, an extraordinary thing happens: a character on screen (Ilsa) conducts a conversation with a character out of frame (Rick), while two other on-screen characters look on. Rick here is so far to the left of the frame that he really is out of the picture. Ilsa is in the position of security, with husband to her right. The whole sequence is overlaid with ironic overtones, culminating in the final look offscreen of Ilsa to Rick which accompanies Renault's naïve (or knowing?) comment that we have Ilsa to thank for making Rick almost human.

Now for a more detailed look at the components of mise-en-scène.

SETTING

Setting is much more than the locations used in a film. It has first of all, a narrative function. In *Casablanca*, the plot is premised on the setting being a place where people are imprisoned, and from which they want to escape. Being in Casablanca is the motor, in effect, for all of the action.

In 1941 the city itself was in an ambivalent geo-political position: it was technically part of Free France, i.e. it hadn't been invaded by the Germans, unlike northern France and in particular, Paris. The Germans, on invading the country, had allowed a puppet government, led by First World War hero Marshal Petain, to administer the country from Vichy, a town much further to the south than Paris. Casablanca, in French Morocco, was governed from Vichy but the ineffectual nature of Vichy France is embodied by its craven prefect of police, and effective governor, Captain Renault.

Casablanca is thus a haven for escaping émigrés and underground resistance leaders but, as it is neither neutral nor under free Allied control, living there is hazardous. The arrival of Major Strasser, who pulls Renault's strings, signifies the knife-edge existence that any enemy of the Third Reich must endure. All of this, of course, makes Casablanca an ideal place in which to set a film about political intrigue and doomed romance.

The principal locations used in the film are limited. This was due to a number of factors: first, the film is based on the script for a stage play, which would inevitably limit the scope for changes of location. Second, the film was made while America was at war, and all the Hollywood studios, Warner Bros most of all, became very strict about production costs. Warner Bros was also well known as the studio most keen to curb production costs and least likely to go in for location shooting. Finally, the nature of the drama demanded a feeling of claustrophobia, a sense that once in Casablanca there was little one could do to escape. A brief look at the significant locations in the film will reinforce this.

The majority of the film is shot inside Rick's Café Americain – either in the main bar area, the casino, or the office upstairs. The bar scenes are dimly or unevenly lit, and tightly framed – to hide cheap and unconvincing sets as much as to connote immobility and claustrophobia. The scenes in the empty bar late at night, and in the office upstairs – when Ilsa comes to Rick on two separate occasions – are where we become intimate with Rick. Downstairs he is the comfortable and secure patron; when the bar is empty and dark he becomes unravelled and vulnerable. Only Sam and Ilsa meet him upstairs. It's an inner sanctum of sorts, though the fact that we never see where he 'lives' (if he has a home other than the bar) suggests that we'll never get too close to him.

The other space in the bar – the roulette room – is closely policed by Rick. He won't let the director of the Deutsche Bank play his tables, and the

mise-en-scène

function of settings

Nazi officers never venture in there. It is only the corrupt Renault and the slippery Ugarte who can come and go as they please.

Though most of the film is set in the bar, there are a few scenes shot outside it. There are only four outdoor scenes in all – the opening sequence, the scene on the café terrace between Rick and Renault, the scene in the bazaar between Rick and Ilsa, and the final scene at the airport. Each has its own narrative and symbolic function.

The opening establishes the locale – an Arab-African city peopled by expatriates – and is necessary for the action with which the plot is instigated. It is also important as it throws into relief much of the rest of the film, which will be filmed indoors. This has the effect of heightening the claustrophobia central to the film's mood.

The bazaar sequence in the middle of the film is important for other reasons. In order for Rick to be filmed at his most vulnerable, it is necessary that he be on terrain that is either neutral, or unfamiliar. This is why he is at a disadvantage with Ilsa in this scene – it's only one of three scenes where we see him outside of the bar, his natural habitat.

The final scenes at the airport offer a parallel to the opening. Renault again utters the now immortal lines 'round up the usual suspects', but this time it is a cynical exercise that will save both him and Rick, and so we are pleased at the outcome. It is also a location that signifies escape – though not initially that of the protagonist. Outdoors does eventually signify freedom – of different sorts – for the principal characters.

The function of these settings in the narrative should be augmented by an understanding of how they were constructed. The whole film, except for the airport scene, was shot on the Warner Bros lot at Burbank. As was common practice, some sets were re-used from previous films, so the bazaar scenes had featured previously in the Warner Bros film *The Desert Song* (1942), and the Paris railway station had been used months before in *Now, Voyager* (1942).

The shots of the plane leaving Casablanca were filmed at a local airport in Los Angeles, although the final airport scene, with the plane being made ready on the runway, was filmed at the studio, with a cast of midgets from Central Casting famously taking the parts of the airport crew and mechanics, in order to give the effect of scale.

LIGHTING

Lighting can augment setting in a variety of ways, but also has narrative functions, and can be coded as part of the 'realist' set-up of mainstream film. It can be separated into two types of strength or intensity – high or low key – as well as by the source and direction of the key or main lights.

The key light is the main light that illuminates the action. It is supplemented by 'fill' lights in order to remove on-set shadows. A typical lighting set-up will feature two high key lights, plus fill light, in order to construct a 'naturalised' picture, say for a dialogue scene. The idea with this set-up is to disguise the fact that this is a film at all, to reinforce the 'realist' force of it.

Removing the fill light, and dimming or reducing the key lights, will create a scene much more unevenly lit, with strong shadows. For a long time in Hollywood cinema it was held as a rule that a frame should not contain any negative – i.e. unlit – space. However, a group of émigré directors and cinematographers arrived in Hollywood from Europe in the 1930s with experience of a different film making aesthetic – German Expressionism. Films made in Germany in the 1920s, like *The Cabinet of Dr Caligari* (1919), *Nosferatu* (1922), and *M* (1931), demonstrated a way of making cinema more risky, artistic, and experimental, summed up in that word 'expressionist'. These film-makers – who included a marginal Michael Curtiz – brought their new aesthetic to Hollywood, and influenced the development of two genres in particular – the horror film, and the film noir.

Casablanca is in many ways expressionist in its lighting. The key scenes are those in the empty bar and in the office above the bar, where Rick is plunged deep into a symbolic darkness, and the use of the searchlights raking the sky and scanning the café. Rick and Renault's conversation early in the film on the terrace of the bar is punctuated by the searchlight, a constant reminder of the threat of war – both for the inhabitants of Casablanca, and the audience.

CINEMATOGRAPHY

It is difficult to disengage lighting from the broader concept of cinematography. Cinematography has been called the art of painting with light. It includes all aspects of camerawork – the set-ups, the depth of field, managing camera movement, and lighting what the camera sees.

Casablanca's cinematographer, Arthur Edeson, was one of the founder members of the American Society of Cinematographers, set up in 1919 (Harmetz, 1993). He was an innovator, learning his craft at a time when the possibilities of what the camera could do were being developed at their most fertile phase, and he had experimented with different lenses and exposures for *The Thief of Baghdad* (1924). Far from being a pictorial stylist, though, Edeson's emphasis was always on how the camerawork could enhance the story and the actors. Harmetz quotes him as saying 'if the lighting and composition are kept as simple and the accent is placed on the story and actors rather than on the camera, we can't go very far wrong.'

In *Casablanca*, Edeson knew to film the opening sequence in an objective, realist style; when it came to the stars, though, he knew how to glamorise, and to soften. David O. Selznick, whose 'property' Ingrid Bergman was, is quoted, again in Harmetz, as being grateful to Edeson for his filming of her. In 1942 Bergman was only on the verge of becoming a big star; her Oscar winning performance in *For Whom the Bell Tolls* was a couple of years away. Edeson's filming of her, with gauze filters over the camera lens, made her glow in a way that helped establish her persona as an other-worldly beauty.

Edeson's wasn't the only influence on the 'look' of *Casablanca*. Hal Wallis had an eye for technical detail that was very rare in a producer. He is credited with complementing Edeson's work on faces, and delicate nuances of shadow, by insisting on darkening the interior of Rick's café. Edeson's

The clever use of lighting
creates delicate nuances
of shadow

wide shots of the bar revealed too much – too much detail, and too much of the cheap set. 'I am anxious to get real blacks and whites, with the walls and the backgrounds in shadow, and dim, sketchy lighting,' Wallis wrote in a memo to Edeson (Harmetz, p. 136).

editing

If mise-en-scène is one way in which cinematic space is constructed for an audience, then editing is just as important. Without editing, the action in a scene can only be shown from one perspective. In early cinema this use of mise-en-scène – the 'proscenium shot' – reproduced the viewpoint an audience might have in a theatre. The camera was positioned directly opposite the action, and all the action happened within that frame. This made certain perspectives impossible, for example the aerial view, the close-up, and the viewpoint of different characters. It also made the transition to a new scene or location difficult, and the cutting between action happening in different places simultaneously impossible.

The dominant system of editing in mainstream cinema is called classic continuity editing. The pioneer was an early American film maker called Edwin S. Porter who established the beginnings of a grammar for the way shots could be stitched together in order to tell a narrative. The conventions or rules by which films are edited are now naturalised to the extent that it is difficult to see how they form or express a system at all, but a look at some of these rules will illustrate how editing is an arbitrary system.

The techniques which comprise classic continuity editing include:

- shot-reverse shot, for shooting conversations
- the close-up for identifying detail
- the point of view shot

In order that cuts from one view to another wouldn't confuse, a set of subsidiary practices have evolved: the 180° rule, which prevented the camera from crossing an invisible line drawn through the action; the 30° rule, which meant that two successive shots of the same object or action must vary in angle by more than 30°. This is probably easier to illustrate than explain:

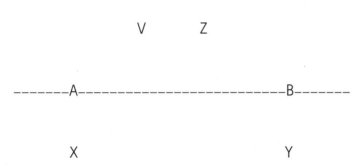

In the diagram above camera X is filming actor B, who is having a conversation with actor A. Camera position Y is used to film actor A when she speaks or responds to what actor B is saying. If some of the conversation were filmed instead from camera position V or Z, the actor would appear on the opposite side of the screen if they were being filmed from X or Y; both actors would appear on either the left or the right hand side of the screen. The effect would disorientate the viewer – their sense of the cinematic space would be disrupted.

Similarly, if actor A is filmed by camera Y, and then the next shot is taken from a camera position a few feet to either side, the viewer would again be confused; why the change of position? The cut in effect would be 'unmotivated' – there would be no clear reason for it, unless it signalled the viewpoint of a new character.

The idea of 'motivation' in editing is another feature of the classic continuity system. In order that the transition between shots be as invisible as possible, so the audience isn't jerked out of their experience of viewing the film, cuts between shots have to have a reason rooted in the film 'world'.

The clearest example is perhaps when sound is used to motivate a cut. A shot of a character together with the sound of glass being broken will arouse in us the desire to see the source of the sound. If we cut next to a

editing

shot of a gloved hand opening a door through a broken pane of glass, we make the connection, and our desire to see the source of the sound is satisfied. We don't question the cut to another shot.

Sound can also be used to bridge shot transitions, the most common example being a piece of music or voice-over that accompanies a montage of images each separate from each other in time and space. In Martin Scorsese's film *New York, New York* (1977), there is a sequence – a 'summary' (see Narrative and form: Time and narrative) – where the heroine sings a song on the soundtrack which accompanies a series of shots of newspaper pages each featuring reviews of her growing success as a singer. Her rise to fame is thus charted in a few shots, and given coherence by the soundtrack.

Another aspect of the grammar of continuity editing is the convention of moving from long, to medium to close-up shot when introducing a new scene. The long shot which starts a scene – or more commonly a film – is called an establishing shot, because it establishes the place, and sometimes the time, of action.

A cut to an interior, maybe bridged by a sound we presume to come from inside, will introduce us to the characters who will be featuring in this scene or action, and we will see them maybe in long shot, then cut to medium shot if they are talking.

In order to follow the conversation, we expect to see their faces a little more closely; if the action has a dramatic effect on one or more of them, then the director will cut to a close-up, and if the action is pivotal, then it is likely that we will cut to an extreme close-up.

In thinking about these conventions it is important to remember a couple of things. First, rules are made to be broken, even within mainstream film. Thus a director like Martin Scorsese will bend or subvert convention, especially in editing, for specific effects. It is also important to remember that these systems were established as common practice by the coming of the sound film; since then audiences have become gradually more literate in their understanding of film language, and consequently film grammar has become more and more abbreviated. The sequence of shots outlined above would seem incredibly tedious and elongated to a modern audience.

A final category of film editing is in the nature of transition from one shot to another.

■ The most common is the standard cut; if a cut isn't motivated, it might be called a jump cut.

■ Dissolves or fades are used to signify the passing of time. A dissolve is a fade-out shot superimposed over a fade-in shot.

■ A fade to black will happen at the end of a discrete sequence of action, as a kind equivalent of the end of an Act in the theatre.

sound

Sound is the third important code in filmmaking, and the one most often overlooked in film analysis. Film is seen as being primarily a visual medium, and the kudos in film appreciation more often goes to the writer, director, or cinematographer than to the sound editor. Walter Murch, the greatest sound editor of his, or maybe of any, generation has noted that 'the analysis of sound in films has always been peculiarly elusive and problematical' (Chion, 1994, p. viii). This is perhaps reasonable; synchronised sound and image only came to the cinema in 1927. To listen to Murch on his work on, for example, *The Conversation* (1974), or *Apocalypse Now* (1979), however, is to come to an understanding of the integral contribution the sound designer or editor makes to patterns of film meaning.

A simple formulaic approach to the analysis of sound in films can be undertaken by looking at a set of categories. First of all there is the distinction between diegetic and non-diegetic sound. The term diegetic (explained in Narrative and form) refers to any element of the film which is within the film-world. Thus diegetic sound refers to dialogue, music (played or performed), sound effects which are sourced directly in the film, either on- or off-screen. Non-diegetic sound is any sound which is imported to the film from an external source, including soundtrack music and voice-over.

sound

performed music

The techniques of sound recording have obviously become more sophisticated since *Casablanca* was made: now the majority of mainstream films record diegetic sound after filming, in a technique known as post-synchronised dubbing. Dialogue is recorded afterwards and added to the film, so that it can be recorded in a controlled environment. Recording diegetic sound on set, on the other hand, tends to be the preserve of either low budget films, like *The Blair Witch Project* (1999), or films looking for a documentary vérité feel, like the films made under the Dogme Manifesto rules.

The sound – particularly the music – in *Casablanca* is a particularly potent source of the film's power and meaning. In fact, it has even been suggested that there is so much performed music in the film that it could almost qualify as a musical. There are over twenty separate sequences of performed music in the film: ten numbers performed by Sam in the café; the 'Marseillaise' and 'Watch on the Rhine'; five numbers that Sam performs for either Rick or Ilsa, or both of them, as in the Paris sequence; and the solos performed by Corinna Mura.

The performed music does much more than add colour and texture to scenes; the thoughtfully chosen songs played by Sam comment on the action and add counterpoint. 'It Had to Be You', 'Speak to Me of Love', and 'If I Could Be with You One Hour Tonight', each have a poignant and ironic resonance when placed next to Rick and Ilsa's relationship.

The musical star of the show is, of course, 'As Time Goes By', and its reluctant star-maker was the Warner Bros in-house composer, Max Steiner. Steiner, another émigré from Europe, was the master of the melodramatic score. Like others who worked on the film he was steeped in his craft; he is credited as being the composer who re-introduced the musical soundtrack to films after the coming of sound. Silent films had always been accompanied by live music; when synchronised sound recording became established (by Warner Bros, incidentally) in 1927, for a while the excitement was all about dialogue and performance. Steiner, in his score for *King Kong* (1933), filled out seventy of the ninety minutes with background music, and thus re-established the art of the film score.

The role of the musical score is crucial in one genre in particular: the melodrama. (For more on *Casablanca*'s relationship to the melodrama see Contexts: Genre.)

The role of melodrama is to express emotional truths in extra-linguistic ways. It has been identified as a genre which appeals to women – hence the strong roles for women in typical melodramas, the narratives which focus on the struggles strong women have to endure, the themes of family and domesticity, romance. The signifying power of the melodrama is reinforced by key elements of cinema – the mise-en-scène and the use of sound. The idea is that in seeking to express very powerful feelings and emotions, dialogue is just not adequate. A whole symphony of cinematic effects have to be mobilised to articulate the language of the heart.

The most powerful melodramas of the 1940s – *Now, Voyager* (1942), *Mildred Pierce* (1945), and *Casablanca* (if it can be called a straight melodrama, which is debatable) were not only produced by Warner Bros, they were also scored by Steiner. One of Steiner's skills was in taking a theme – either one 'on loan' as it were, or one he had composed himself – and modulating it rapidly through different registers and moods. Thus in *Mildred Pierce,* for example, he can, in less than a minute, take a musical theme and transform it to connote optimism, threat, tragic pity, and reconciliation.

This is the kind of operation that characterises Steiner's work on *Casablanca.* His score not only modulates around 'As Time Goes By' (a song he famously resisted using, thinking he could write something better himself); it also weaves in and out of the 'Marseillaise' and 'Deutschland Uber Alles'. Thus he synthesises, in musical terms, the two major strands of the film – the romance and the political intrigue.

contexts

ideology *p60*   production history *p66*   genre *p71*   audience *p79*
intertextuality *p82*   the film spectator *p87*

ideology

The term ideology has a long and complex provenance in the study of film. In its (over) simplest form, it relates to the ways in which meanings and values, current in a particular society at a given time, are reproduced in a particular film. Of course, any society will circulate a wide range of beliefs and values: some will be dominant – that is given wide credence, perhaps to the extent that they are seen to represent 'common-sense' views of the way the world is. Others will be held by marginal groups, and either be resistant or subversive.

In Western democracies, the relationship between dominant and marginal, or resistant beliefs or values, will be under constant negotiation; dominant value systems function more successfully if scope is allowed for alternatives, so outright repression will be rare.

Media products, like films, newspapers or advertisements, are often taken to be the places where this negotiation is made manifest. Study of the kinds of values, messages, groups and individuals that media products represent, will reveal how ideologies operate, combine and conflict. Indeed, the concept of 'representation' is traditionally where media studies, and branches of film studies address the workings of ideology.

REPRESENTATION

One of the keys to the success of *Casablanca* is the range on offer of representations of both groups and individuals. Anthony Heilbut (in Harmetz, 1992) has speculated that the film might be an expression of the 'émigré sensibility' because of the high proportion of European actors featured on the cast list (see Background: Key players' biographies).

The use of 'European-ness' in the film fulfils a number of functions. Laszlo's idealism and nobility is enhanced by Paul Henreid's background as

60   CASABLANCA **y**

upper/middle-class Austrian, playing a Czech Resistance leader. This, in turn, draws on Warner Bros's experience of producing biopic films covering the lives of European radicals and visionaries.

The films *The Story of Louis Pasteur* (1936), and *The Life of Emile Zola* (1937), presented portrayals of radical European men, unafraid of challenging dominant and conservative social and establishment forces, and there is something of those characters in the admittedly sketchily drawn Victor Laszlo.

Europeans in American culture have traditionally represented complex sets of values and ideas. On the one hand, Europe stands for a delicate and refined sensibility; think of the enthusiasm with which Americans tour European countries, in search of sophistication, history, and culture. On the other, there is the tradition of the European man in particular representing a threat to innocent American women abroad. The novels of Henry James often revolve around devious and superficially attractive European men damaging ingenuous American women abroad.

'Englishness' in American culture inhabits something of this place, too. The suave Sydney Greenstreet was used repeatedly in Warner Bros films for the edgy and slightly sinister sophistication he brought to parts. And Claude Rains's charm – facile and weak, though ultimately grounded in 'civilised' values – worked perfectly in the role of Renault, the vacillating prefect of police.

The American perception of European sophistication was responsible in no small part for the rewriting of easy-loving American Lois into the character of the noble, impressionable, Norwegian Ilsa Lund. Ingrid Bergman – relatively fresh to American screens – brought a European glamour and nobility to the part. When she left her husband and started an affair with Italian director Roberto Rossellini – bearing his child – the fall from grace in American public opinion was doubly fierce because of the connotations she had previously brought to the parts she played.

In the midst of this, two American characters stand out – Rick and Sam. Sam's role as black character, improbable as it may seem, advanced the roles for black actors in Hollywood. Even though, typically, his part is the servant and entertainer to white America, he still has important moments

propaganda film

in the film, and is obviously loved and respected by his boss, and our point of identification, Rick. He has a key narrative role as the connection between Rick and Ilsa, and has some great comic lines.

The *Variety* review of the film singled Dooley Wilson out for special mention from among the 'lesser characters', compounding this misapprehension by pointing out that he was 'a Negro'. The stereotype of the black entertainer is reinforced by references solely to Wilson's musical role, mistakenly thinking into the bargain that he actually played the piano in the film, and neglecting to comment on his acting.

Rick himself clearly represents the image America would like to have of itself. Self-reliant, careful of his trust, with a core of decency which had been broken by what he thinks is a faithless (European) woman, Rick is the repository of American ideals, hopes, and beliefs.

As this was meant to be a propaganda film, however, his position is complicated. His radical idealism is represented as being threateningly isolationist in a world that needs the engagement of resourceful men; this was mirrored in a very real isolationist mood abroad in America at the time. Not until the Japanese attacked Pearl Harbor on 7 December 1941, did the mood begin to change.

In a narrative resolution that Robert Ray feels (1985) enabled America to preserve its individuality, while still doing its duty, Rick's exit from Casablanca signifies America's 'avoidance of choice'. A decision is made, action is taken, but the hero is then free to retreat to another scenario; he does not have to see anything through.

HEGEMONY AND NARRATIVE

Study of the *content* of media products, however, is only the starting point for a study of ideology. Writers have progressed beyond this to look at the *form* of principally film, in order to address the 'how' of ideology – drawing on the work of the thinkers Althusser, Gramsci, and Freud. What follows is not a direct account of the influence of any of these writers; for that, readers will have to go elsewhere (for example, Nelmes, 1999 or 1994; Cook, 1999 or 1996). Instead, here is a potted digest of key ideas relating to the workings of ideology in film.

perception of European sophistication

ideology

The mechanism by which democratic societies manage the range of conflicting values and beliefs which are at large, was named 'hegemony' by the Italian Marxist, Antonio Gramsci. Hegemony is a dynamic by which an equilibrium is maintained in society: enough of marginal or alternative voices are allowed to be heard, but they are framed and contained within dominant forms and forces. Outright repression is never necessary; by keeping subversion expressed marginally, what is dominant is always coded as 'normal' or 'natural'. This is an approach that can be taken to the workings of texts.

In soap-opera, for example, conflicting representations of women are offered to us. We have female characters who suffer, sacrifice, and struggle – particularly middle-aged, working-class women. To glamorise these characters and present them as happy-go-lucky people would strain the credulity of audiences; on the other hand, to present them relentlessly in a negative light would remove much of the pleasure of identifying with them and turn audiences off.

What results, then, is a kind of balance wherein these women have their own triumphs and moments of glory, but are never allowed to leave the situations they are in. The narrative structure which allows this might be called 'hegemonic'.

Casablanca balances its own conflicting forces in a similar way. The major conflict of values is between the isolationist and individualist American philosophy of life, and a wider set of humanist values, to do with sacrificing one's own desires for the sake of the wider community. This conflict is explicitly dealt with in the character of Rick.

The early introductory scenes, featuring Rick, reveal a man who sticks his neck out for nobody. He does not associate with the patrons of his bar, and forms no permanent attachments with women (such as Yvonne, dropped ruthlessly after a brief affair). In short, he is fiercely independent.

There is, however, enough material early on, for us to form a view of him having become this way because he has been damaged by disappointments in the past. He has left his native America for shadowy reasons; he has a track-record of supporting underdogs – in Ethiopia and Spain. It is also clear that he has a core of decency: he refuses the money of the German banker in the casino, is disdainful of Ugarte's exploitation of human traffic, and actively tries to thwart Renault's abuse of vulnerable women. These contradictions are set up in his character from the beginning, then, which only the arrival of Ilsa at the bar, and the subsequent flashback scenes can begin to explain.

In one sense, the resolving of these contradictions is the true narrative of *Casablanca*: will the core of decency be re-awakened? Or will the impossibility of renewing his relationship with Ilsa cause him to retreat further into his shell? Typically, in terms of the hegemonic management of the narrative, a balance is arrived at, in which he neither allows himself to be co-opted completely to the cause, nor absolutely rejects it. He is allowed one noble act – the killing of Strasser and the relinquishing of Ilsa – in support of the Allied cause, but still maintains his independence in his final exit with Renault.

The film also balances conflicting versions of gender roles. The women play stereotypical functional gender roles, with little opportunity to shape the narrative or become individuated in complex ways. Ilsa is little more than an icon of beauty; her function in the film is as a site of visual pleasure, with her glowing, natural, almost virginal looks. At crucial points she relinquishes any power she might have: it is Rick who has to 'do the thinking for both of us, for all of us'.

The look of bewilderment in the final scene – reinforced by stories that Bergman genuinely did not know which man she was to leave with – is this dis-empowerment made visual. Two men are about to act in different directions while she looks on helplessly. Even so, she does have two scenes of potential decisiveness – in the bazaar and in the upstairs office.

In the first, the source of her power over Rick is actually in the fact that she is married – and so, ironically, powerless to act. In the second, she draws a gun, in an image that would be replicated in many film noirs of the 1940s. Unlike the femme fatale, however, who actually uses the gun in decisive narrative moments, Ilsa is unable to pull the trigger, instead falling into Rick's arms. Rick, in the end, is the only character who can use the gun to decisive effect.

The other female roles are similarly feckless or powerless. Annina, the Bulgarian wife, is defined by the needs of her husband. When faced with the one opportunity to act decisively – by sleeping with Renault she will 'earn' a safe passage to Lisbon – she instead turns to Rick who sorts out the situation for her. To audiences at the time, this would have made Rick seem heroic; to later feminist critics, it would seem like a patronising removal of the woman's one decisive course of action.

Similarly Yvonne is presented as acted upon, rather than as a decisive agent. She is spurned by Rick in the early scenes, takes up with the Nazi enemy, then returns to the cause during the singing of the 'Marseillaise': another example of feckless woman.

It is not surprising, in view of the time, that the decisive agents in the film are all men. Laszlo is the source of hopes and ideals in the film; Ilsa merely echoes and supports them. One could argue, of course, that Laszlo's idealist stance is naive. While he is away at a resistance meeting, Ilsa is reduced to having to compromise her moral self by offering to sleep with Rick in return for the letters of transit. Annina, too, is faced with the same type of choice. It is as if the idealist men are like children, who have to be protected from the kind of difficult choices faced constantly by women.

Renault acts out a more ambivalent gender role. Though an active agent, his actions are circumscribed by his political situation and his own weakness for women. He says at one point that he blows with the wind, and that the prevailing wind is coming from Vichy. His relationship to Strasser is one of dignified pragmatic obedience. The persona of the actor, Claude Rains, was one of silver-tongued charm, and this, combined with his height (he was shorter than both Bergman and Bogart) made him unsuitable to play a romantic leading man.

The American tradition for male heroes was for them to be reticent, slightly disdainful and aloof, and rarely revealing vulnerability. They also had to be American. Rains was always cast, therefore, in supporting character roles.

In Hitchcock's *Notorious* (1946), he finally gets to bed and wed Ingrid Bergman, but for her it is a marriage of convenience. In *Now, Voyager*

(1942), made immediately before *Casablanca*, he plays Bette Davis's wise and kindly psychiatrist, while she falls in love with Paul Henreid. It is not straining credibility too far to suggest, as one critic has done, that Renault's and Rick's is the true love story – in which Renault's is the feminised character, galvanised into action and decision by the example of the tough guy.

production history

A more focused or grounded approach to the ideological concerns of a film can be made by looking at the specific circumstances in which it was made. For a studio film made in Hollywood in 1942, this would have to take into account the following: censorship; the social and cultural climate at the time; system of production. Of these, the last has been dealt with in Background and will not need recapping here. But some more detail is needed on what was happening in America – and the rest of the world – in 1942.

HOLLYWOOD AT WAR

The day of 8 December 1941 – when the script of *Everybody Comes to Rick's* landed on Hal Wallis's desk – turned out to be an important one for the careers of the major players involved in the film. The day before, however, was even more momentous: on Sunday, 7 December, America was woken out of its complacent observation of the two-year-old war in Europe by the bombing of its major Pacific naval base at Pearl Harbor, Hawaii. This single action pushed America into the war – and Hollywood mobilised along with the rest of the country.

Up to this point, Hollywood's position *vis-à-vis* the Allied cause in Europe had been ambivalent. There was a strong American-German lobby, composed of earlier generations of immigrants to America, and sensitivity to its feelings was such that, in 1938, the Hays Office could object to Warner Bros's negative portrayal of Hitler in *Confessions of a Nazi Spy.*

In addition to these tensions over relations with Germany, there was also the fact that Hollywood was a liberal community in a country which then, as now, had powerful right-wing Republican voices. The Warners, particularly Jack, were very pro-Roosevelt, the Democrat president during the Depression and the war, to the extent that they could be fairly accused of sanctifying him in the crude propaganda piece *Mission to Moscow* (1943).

Warner Bros, in fact, had a tradition of supporting the urban underclass, and the underdog in general. Of all the big movie mogul families, the four Warner brothers, the sons of a Russian-Jewish immigrant shoe-mender in Ohio, had risen the highest. By 1940, the production studio was run by Harry and Jack, very different temperamentally, but together on politics. Their positions were reflected in the films they made – often hard-hitting gritty realist dramas set among the disenfranchised and made for audiences with similar backgrounds to their own.

Their frugality was legendary, and mixed with a reluctance to pamper their stars. When the war came, and economies had to be made, Warner Bros were ready to respond with vigour – and to make publicity out of it. In *Casablanca,* Ingrid Bergman wore the first all-cotton film costume, as wool and silk had been banned.

The sets – like Bryan Foy's scripts (see Genre) – were recycled from earlier projects, where possible. The set for the bazaar scene, for example, is taken from *The Desert Song* (1942), which had just finished filming, and the Parisian railway station is the same station set used in *Now, Voyager* (1942). In all, the set cost $18,000, which is remarkable because there were only two scenes shot outside the studio – the arrival of Major Strasser, and some night shots of planes taxiing on a runway – both shot at a local provincial airport.

Shortly after the war started, there were several institutional pressures on Hollywood studios to make films which supported the war effort. The Hays Office, which administered the Motion Picture Production Code (or Hays Code), was still active. The government had set up the Office of War Information (OWI) – a propaganda office given the task of persuading men to join up, and everybody to support the war effort.

The OWI made increasingly strenuous efforts to shape the content of Hollywood films, but had no statutory power; the only direct pressure the government could put on the studios was to prevent – via the Office of Censorship – the export of movies of which it disapproved. Thus, early on after the release of *Casablanca*, prints of the film were withheld from North Africa lest the Vichy government in France be offended.

The strictures of the OWI included a 'manual' setting out how films could support the war effort. This expanded, in bureaucratic style, to include a range of different sections and sub-sections. The main headings covering the approved content of war films were:

I. THE ISSUES – Why we fight. What kind of peace will follow victory.

II. THE ENEMY – Whom we fight. The nature of our adversary.

III. The UNITED NATIONS AND PEOPLES – With whom we are allied in fighting. Our brothers in arms.

IV. WORK AND PRODUCTION – How each of us can fight. The war at home.

V. THE HOME FRONT – What we must do. What we must give up to win the fight.

VI. THE FIGHTING FORCES – The job of the fighting man at the Front.

Films made in Hollywood were reviewed by the Bureau of Motion Pictures, set up by the OWI to monitor and pressurise film-makers. The Bureau assessed new films according to the headings in the manual and, not surprisingly, gave *Casablanca* the all-clear. Its themes of self-sacrifice and duty, its critical portrayal of isolationism, and its representation of America as a safe haven of civilised values, made it entirely supportive of the Allied war effort.

This was hardly surprising as Warner Bros were the first in the queue when it came to war patriotism. Their support for Roosevelt and his New Deal liberalism is also reflected in the film. Rick is a sympathetic employer, and his staff are dignified. There is no hint of racial or social tensions in the café; it is only the unscrupulous Sydney Greenstreet who tries to buy Sam.

production history

CENSORSHIP

The other direct indicator of social and political climate impacting on film is that of formal censorship. In Hollywood between 1922 and the early 1950s there was a strictly enforced censorship system, ostensibly self-regulatory, but one which studio personnel either kicked against or circumvented.

From 1922, regulation of the content of Hollywood films was managed by the Motion Picture Producers and Distributors of America (MPPDA), whose president was ex-Republican politician Will Hays. He gave his name to both the office and the code of practice which the MPPDA was responsible for administering. By 1934, considerable pressure from outside agencies – including a boycott of cinemas by Pennsylvania Catholics – prompted the major studios to submit film content to formal censorship.

The Production Code was administered by the Production Code Administration (PCA), and by 1942 its chief was Joseph Breen. Film scripts, as well as the final cut version of the film, had to be cleared with the PCA. The Code contained many strictures about the portrayal of religion, crime, foreign nationals and governments.

Most famously, the Code's strictures concerned sex – or its absence – on screen. Adult nudity was absolutely forbidden; kisses were only allowed to a last a few seconds; bedrooms had to be represented carefully, and certainly not as the site of sexual activity. When a woman kissed a man, she had to keep one foot on the floor. Of most pertinence to *Casablanca* were the Code references to 'impure love', that is, sex outside marriage. While reference to adulterous liaisons was allowed, it was clear that those engaged in it were not to profit from, nor find happiness in it.

The original stage-play script of *Everybody Comes to Rick's* was, in the words of the first Warner Bros reader, 'highly censorable'. Lois (the prototype of Ilsa) was clearly someone who was casual about her relationships with men, and Renault (or Rinaldi, as he was originally) equally apparently sold visas for sexual favours. When the script was submitted to the PCA, its head, Joe Breen, wrote back a series of amendments:

Specifically we cannot approve the present suggestion that Capt. Renault makes a practice of seducing the women to whom he grants visas. Any such inference of illicit sex could not be approved in the finished picture ...

Page 86: The suggestion that Ilsa was married all the time she was having her affair with Rick in Paris seems unacceptable, and could not be approved in the finished picture. Hence we request the deletion of the line 'Even when I knew you in Paris.'

With a view to removing the now offensive characterisation of Renault as an immoral man who engages himself in seducing women to whom he grants visas, it has been agreed with Mr. Wallis that the several references to this particular phase of the gentleman's character will be materially toned down, to-wit:

Page 5: The line in scene 15 'The girl will be released in the morning' will be changed to the expression 'Will be released later ...'

Page 75: ... the word 'joy' in Renault's line is to be changed to the word 'like'. 'you like war. I like women.'

Page 76: Renault's line 'At least your work keeps you outdoors' is to be changed to 'Gets you plenty of fresh air.'

from Behlmer, 1986

These requests reveal an alarming sensitivity to language and nuance. The switch from 'joy' to 'like' is particularly inexplicable. The finished version of the film demonstrates how film language had to accommodate the strictures of the Code and become more ingenious at signifying illicit behaviour outside language. It also explains Ilsa's clumsy explanation to Rick about her marriage to Laszlo, and how she had thought him dead until the day before they were due to leave Paris.

Finally, it explains that infamous dissolve in the scene in the upstairs office. The PCA could not object to it implying a sexual liaison, because nothing was shown. Here, elegantly, the absence of an action implies its actual occurrence, and only if the PCA were post-structuralists, three decades early, could they have objected.

genre

In fact, Richard Maltby (1995) notes that ambiguity is one of the key tropes and appeals of *Casablanca*. Audiences are invited to fill in a number of gaps in the film by using their imagination. Some events are either mentioned but not represented, like Ugarte's death (suicide – or killed resisting arrest?), and Rick's past. Others, like Annina's 'bad thing', are implied but never happen; and still others, like the dissolve in the office, are implied but not shown.

Maltby says that – due to the practice of 'delicate indication' – the Hays Office was partly responsible for this ambiguity. It is as if they secretly sanctioned the presence or trace of impropriety, but not its portrayal.

genre

One of the conundrums posed by *Casablanca* is the question of its generic position. Is it a war film? A melodrama? A romantic thriller? Is there sufficient music for it to qualify as a musical? Other interesting possibilities are that it bears similarities to the classic Hollywood Western (Ray, 1985), and that it contains overtones of the biopics which Warner Bros produced in the 1930s.

One commentator on the film, Umberto Eco (1987), puts the film's appeal down to the fact that it transcends any single generic category – it contains the central elements of a million stories we have heard or seen before, from a whole range of genres. Before embarking on a closer generic analysis of the film, however, it would be wise to survey the concept of film genre itself.

GENRE AND CRITICISM

Traditionally, accounts of film genres separate at least three different sources for the idea of genre. First, there is genre criticism in which writers and academics attempt to characterise single or multiple genres by setting out a typology (that is, a list of characteristic features or elements which any single genre should contain). In addition, genre critics may hypothesise a set of reasons why genres – in film and other aspects of culture – exist at all.

problems of analysing film

The anthropologist Claude Levi-Strauss maintained that different cultures had a set of stories in common, whose origin was in the patterns of the human mind. Other critics have developed Levi-Strauss's binary structures to postulate that genres effectively are means of society dealing with opposition and conflict which, in reality, are irresolvable.

Genre critics have suggested that genres follow typical patterns of development, for example from a prototype, through a classic, and into a revisionist and even a decadent phase (see Altman, 1999). The film critic Thomas Schatz (in Nelmes, 1999 or 1996) has even distinguished between two types of genre – those of 'order' (the Western, gangster, and sci-fi film) and those of 'integration' (the musical, the melodrama, the romantic comedy).

The inherent differences rest in the fact that in genres of order, the focus is on the struggle for justice of a lone male against a corrupt institution – a struggle which ends in a violent resolution and which renders the hero an outcast from the society he is trying to save. In genres of integration, the focus is on the struggle of a community, or of a woman within a community, to achieve a harmonious balance of its conflicting tensions and needs, a struggle which ends happily, often in marriage.

Elegant though these categorisations may be, however, there are real problems with genre criticism as a form of analysis of film. Firstly, these categorisations are all post-hoc – that is, they benefit from a hindsight which sees similarities between films, whereas when they were made, they may have been categorised very differently.

A second difficulty is that, before deciding what the features of any single genre may include, one has to choose a set of films which may belong to the genre. In fact, as Andrew Tudor (quoted in Cook, 1999 or 1994) has pointed out, this can lead to deciding what the genre is before setting about identifying it.

An example which illustrates some of the problems of using genre as a way of analysing film is cited by Richard Maltby (1995). Film noir was a phrase coined by French film critics in the 1950s following the release of a successful series of crime novels, translated in France from their American originals. The title 'Serie Noir' came to be transposed on to a type of film made in Hollywood between 1945 and 1955, which were characterised by strong use of shadow, plots concerning a doomed central protagonist, and a central female character who was scheming and sexy (called, in another echo of the French provenance of the genre, a 'femme fatale').

However, Maltby says, what are retrospectively called films noir actually at the time were categorised by the studios under maybe half-a-dozen different categories, like the crime film, the crime thriller, the melodrama the social problem film.

To speak of these films, made by different studios, as a coherent group of 'films noir', therefore, is obviously to ignore the conditions in which they were made. And yet, in retrospect, there is a consistency – of narrative, setting, character, and iconography. Subsequently, many film directors have paid homage to the look, the mood, and the philosophy of these films – to the extent that it has now become established as a genre whose makers are consciously following an aesthetic and a pattern (see for example *The Grifters*, 1990; *Blue Velvet*, 1986; *Klute*, 1971; *Deep Cover*, 1992; *The Last Seduction*, 1993).

GENRE AND HOLLYWOOD

A second source of the idea of genre lies in the film industry itself. It was long held as axiomatic that, during the classic Hollywood period, studios knew that, in order to maximise profits, it was sensible to stick with 'tried and tested' film formulae. In effect, this meant limiting any variation to simply satisfying an audience that they had not seen the film before. Thus, the film industry cranked out genre pictures as if they were mass-producing automobiles.

A famous oft-cited story about Bryan Foy, who ran the B-movie unit at Warner Bros in the late 1930s, has him sitting behind a desk on which a huge pile of scripts were stacked. Allegedly, when it was time to put a new film into production, he would take the script off the top of the pile, switch the genre – maybe from a wrestling picture to a racing picture – and a new film would be coined from an old script. In this way, the pile of scripts was constantly recycled. The Coen Brothers' film *Barton Fink* (1991) is based on just such a scenario.

exploiting the talent

Film critics thus legitimated their use of genre as a concept by reference to the fact that it was, supposedly, a key concept and practice in the industry itself.

Recent writing on genre has begun to revise this conception of genre as industry standard, however. Rick Altman, in his book *Film/Genre* (1999), suggests that 'genre' was never an industry term – nor a studio concern. He charts the origin of the titles of major genres – musical, western, comedy – as adjectives describing films, often in hyphenated form, which only later became nouns – the *names* of genres, like Western, Horror, Musical.

Thus, what we know as a Musical might have been called in the trade press at the time a 'musical comedy of manners', or a 'western adventure with a romantic plot'. What Altman suggests is that, once the adjective had turned into a noun, a title, the genre as such had probably run out of steam.

Film production, as Maltby suggests as well, went in short 'cycles' in Hollywood in the 1930s. Thus, what we think of the gangster genre is based on a collection of crime films made by Warner Bros in 1931 and 1932.

The studios were less interested in following a tried-and-tested formula for their A pictures for two reasons. First, they were in competition with other studios – and staying distinctive made economic sense. If they produced high-budget films that had a recognisable and replicable content, then other studios would make money out of their idea. There was no patent on generic formulae. In fact, when a cycle became established and formalised into a genre it had already become hackneyed. The more imitations were made, the less currency the formula had with audiences. Time for the studio to start a new cycle.

The second reason was that studios wanted to foreground the elements which were peculiar to them, things which no one else had. For studios this meant talent – stars, directors, writers. Thus, they were most concerned with exploiting the talent at their disposal, in roles to which they were best suited – and this often, though not always, meant stars appearing in films which were similar to each other. Errol Flynn at

Warner Bros, for example, was obviously best exploited in swashbuckling adventure yarns. This did not limit Warner Bros to making pirate films for him, however; essentially, he played the same role in war films, historical epics, and even Westerns.

Contemporary reviews of *Casablanca* demonstrate Altman's thesis to some degree. The American *Motion Picture Herald* of 28 November 1942 categorised the film as an 'Adult Refugee Drama', while *Variety*, on 2 December 1942 called the film an 'adventure-romance'. Neither of these designations refers to genre names which critics might use later. Likewise, the British magazine *The Cinema* (13 January, 1943) called it a 'political melodrama'. These categories are intended solely as markers for audiences and cinema-bookers of what kind of film to expect; they do not function as critical categories for film academics.

GENRE AND AUDIENCE

The third source for understanding and explaining genre comes with the study of audiences. Audiences, it has been asserted, effectively 'co-produce' the meaning of a genre film by virtue of the fact that we carry round with us a set of expectations of what, say a horror film, a gangster film, a musical, will look and feel like.

For us, part of the pleasure of watching a Western will lie in the anticipation of key generic features: Who will be the bad guy? How will the final shoot-out be managed? How will the hero not get the girl? If any particular Western strayed too far from the generic template, for example by not having a final shoot-out, by not being set in the Wild West in the second half of the last century, or by not featuring a lone hero, then we would be disappointed.

Again, contemporary reviewers of *Casablanca* demonstrate the connection between generic categories and audience expectation. The *Variety* reviewer reminded cinema managers that the film 'goes heavy on the love theme' and that 'adventure is there too, but it's more as exciting background to the Bogart-Bergman heart department'. Bogart clearly already stood for 'high adventure rather than romance', although they pointed out that 'there's plenty of the latter for the *femme* trade'.

potential box-office appeal

GENRE AND CASABLANCA

So how does a genre approach help to explain *Casablanca?* Altman's explanation of the Hollywood studio relationship to genres offers a useful introductory context. Far from being a studio genre product, the origins of *Casablanca* at Warner Bros were first in an opportunist attempt to capitalise on America's entry into the Second World War. This does not mean just that they saw the script of *Everybody Comes to Rick's* as an opportunity to make money out of the prevailing climate; it was more important for Jack Warner, ultimately in charge of production, to make patriotic films that would support the war effort.

In addition, Warner Bros were also looking for story vehicles in which to promote their new rising leading man, Humphrey Bogart. The Rick part was envisaged from the start as Bogart's role, and a chance to enhance and develop the persona he had delivered in *The Maltese Falcon* the year before.

The story itself had a potential box-office appeal in its concerns with sacrifice, romance, and political intrigue. In Altman's terms, then, the focus of the film for Warner Bros was in its tie-in with their proprietary elements – script and star – and with the prevailing social and political climate.

Thirdly, Warner Bros wanted to replicate the success of ensemble cast-pieces starring Bogart, Lorre, Greenstreet, and Rains. The project carried echoes of previous Warner Bros successes – *The Maltese Falcon* (1941), with its similar central character, as well as its potential for using an ensemble cast of strong character actors such as Sydney Greenstreet, Peter Lorre, and Claude Rains.

Across the Pacific (1942), the film Bogart made before *Casablanca,* attempted to re-exploit the principals of *The Maltese Falcon* – and used the same director, John Huston. Indeed, Warner Bros tried to replicate *Casablanca* afterwards – again as a 'package' of talent rather than generically – in *Passage To Marseilles* the year after. The set-up of doomed hero trapped in an exotic North African location had precedents in both *Pepe le Moko* (1937), a French vehicle for current leading man Jean Gabin, and *Pepe* was 'Hollywoodised' in the 1938 film *Algiers. Casablanca*, then is

significant section of cinema culture

not a straightforward genre film in the sense that its contemporary Westerns, gangster films, or musicals were.

However, as mentioned in Narrative and form: Narrative models and their uses, Robert Ray (1985) does see strong parallels in *Casablanca* with Westerns of the same period.

With the classic Western, *Casablanca* shares in common:

■ a lone hero cast outside his 'natural' home and milieu (for Rick this is New York, evidenced by his asking Sam at one point 'If it's midnight here, what time is it in New York?')

■ a love affair with a woman which cannot be sustained; the hero's sympathy with a set of values shared by the audience (sacrifice of love before duty)

■ his opposition to a corrupt authority

■ a resolution of the narrative, and these attendant tensions, through a violent act which renders the hero unable to be incorporated back into civil society.

What these parallels reveal, according to Maltby, is maybe a weakness in genre criticism, namely that Hollywood films in general share so many similarities that categorising them by genre is to reveal only minor differences. Maybe what we think of as genres are really only variants of one small but significant section of cinema culture – the classic Hollywood film.

Casablanca has also been marshalled into service as a 'proto-noir'. This presumably is because of its emphatic lighting system – strong use of shadows, avoidance of daylight, use of interiors. The character of Rick bears superficial similarities with noir protagonists – he is a loner, a cynic who seems to have lost faith with civilised values, and unlucky in love. However, he is redeemed by a renewal of faith in Western liberal values to do with sacrifice, and he rejects the possibility of a relationship with a woman who, no matter how complex she is, is certainly not the scheming nihilistic femme fatale of film noir. In the latter categories – doomed protagonist, and femme fatale – *The Maltese Falcon* has a much stronger claim to prefiguring the film noir of the 1940s.

shares melodramatic style

The film has strong affinities with melodrama. Melodrama itself is a slippery term. In one sense it is not a genre at all, but rather a mode of expression – characterised by heightened appeals to strong emotion – that can be found in an array of genres, like the horror film, the musical, the biopic.

The 'language' of melodrama lies most obviously in the expression of feeling through music, gesture, and mise-en-scène. A scene such as that in *Mildred Pierce* (1945) where Mildred confronts her daughter on the stairs, and slaps and hysterical accusations are exchanged to a background of passionate music, is typical of melodramatic excess.

In its narrower sense, melodrama overlaps with the genre of the 'women's film' of the 1930s and 1940s, which included *Now, Voyager* (1942), *Stella Dallas* (1937), and *Mildred Pierce* (1945). These films featured a strong central female protagonist, someone who endures conflict and tension arising primarily out of her family situation, and who has to sacrifice her own individual desires in order that her family can be reconstituted.

Casablanca apparently shares some of the melodramatic style in its presentation. The 'Marseillaise' sequence is melodramatic in its use of music to mobilise powerful communal feeling, and the use of 'As Time Goes By' does the same to signify powerful feelings in an individual relationship.

Even though the central character is not a woman, Rick has to sublimate his own desires for the sake of a wider community, and in a sense he is a kind of protective matriarch in relation to his staff. However, unlike the resolution to a melodrama, he is not reintegrated into the community, and instead sets out for a new territory.

Is it then a war film? *Casablanca* shares some of the pre-occupations of other films concerned with portraying the current war with Germany. It was intended to mobilise feeling in America in support of the Allied cause by appealing to traditional American values – the role of the individual in safeguarding society's freedoms. But it is not an action film, in the sense that war films of the 1940s were to become when the Office of War Information took a greater role in advising – not to say controlling – film production.

It certainly is a propaganda film – witness the following lines that could have been planted by the equivalent of today's spin doctor: 'I stick my neck out for no-one', 'I bet they're asleep all over America', 'I'm the only cause I'm interested in', 'Isolationism these days, my dear Rick, just isn't an option' – but it does not seek to persuade young men to join up and fight.

If *Casablanca* cannot be slotted into one genre, is this a problem? One possible answer comes from Rick Altman, again. He says that because genres are, after all, categories devised by critics after the films included in them have been made, it is impossible for any single film to be cited as the perfect and complete example of any one genre. In fact, it is far more likely that any single film will contain elements recognisable from a range of genres.

It is easy to see that some films, such as *Oklahoma!* (1955), or *Blazing Saddles* (1974), are generic hybrids (musical-Western, and comedy-Western respectively). With others, such as *Casablanca*, it is harder to fix them because the generic elements are too multiple. His answer for the latter category is the idea of 'multi-valent' or 'multi-vocal' features of films. A single scene in a single film might contain references to a range of genres; or, rather, a single scene may be read, according to the purpose of the viewer, from one of many different generic perspectives.

Casablanca, then, will be classified as classic drama in a video store, or on the cover of its re-released video version. Watched in a history lesson, it becomes a film reflecting the war climate of the early 1940s. In film studies, it serves as a case-study of the persona of Humphrey Bogart, or of the Warner Bros house-style of film production under Hal Wallis. Some sequences use a highly melodramatic style of presentation; others are distinctly noir in lighting style. The plot follows that of other thriller romances. Many scenes can be read from all of these perspectives.

audience

Much of this part of the book has been concerned with factors to do with the way the production of *Casablanca* has shaped the eventual outcome of the film. However, a large and growing component of film studies has focused on a concern with the audiences for films.

group profiles

Initially, the film audience was considered – if at all – to be an unproblematic area, the place where films ended up, having gone through their complex labours. Developments in theory in the 1960s and 1970s, in relation to both film and more widely, media in general, started to introduce the idea that the audience for film might have a more active and central role in the making of meaning.

The influences on these development in the widest sense, are the work of the French psychoanalyst Jacques Lacan, and the Marxist philosopher Louis Althusser; their ideas are too complex to be rehearsed here, and besides, their ideas have been 'cooked' by a group of film theorists, whose work is more central to the account here. The material which follows owes a great deal to Patrick Phillips, author of the section 'The Film Spectator' in *An Introduction to Film Studies* (Nelmes, 1999 or 1996). In that book, Phillips has an extended section on advanced theories of spectatorship, which the reader of this book might want to move on to.

Phillips distinguishes between two ways of approaching the study of how films are watched. On the one hand, there is the film audience – a heterogeneous group of people, each of whom has made an individual decision to come to a cinema and watch the same film. They might come in a group, in a couple, or on their own; they have been exposed to the same marketing campaign – or at the very least, sources of information – promoting the film, but this is not to say that they each come to the film expecting or wanting the same thing.

They sit in an auditorium, in the dark, and experience the same event, though not in the same ways. Their response, pleasure, enjoyment – or lack of it – will be shaped in large part by who they are: their age, gender, ethnic group, sexual orientation; and how they came to be who they are: their personality, personal history, mood and temperament.

THE FILM AUDIENCE

This notion of 'audience', which is current in media studies, is primarily concerned with how audience experience can be looked at in terms of group profiles. In fact, it bears a strong similarity to the ways in which media organisations, film companies included, conceive of their audiences.

audience

Thus, for example, a film company might have particular strategies for selling a film to an audience aged between sixteen and twenty-four – currently the largest target 'demographic' for cinema.

Understandings of audience became more sophisticated when it became clear that just describing the age, ethnicity, gender etc., of a target group would not account for how they responded to or understood a film or other media product. In the media industries this led to a more subtle profiling of groups – like 'psychographic profiling' – particularly in market research and advertising; in media and cultural studies, too, the focus shifted to categorise the different ways an audience might respond. The three major categories devised by critics and academics were 'preferred', 'negotiated', and 'oppositional' readings.

'Preferred' readings, as the name suggests, refers to the possibility that a media product might have one dominant meaning or set of values which it chooses to foreground. In advertising this equates to the USP, or Unique Selling Proposition, that is the single message that an advert must relay for the sake of clarity.

'Oppositional' readings, on the other hand, are those responses to a media product that its makers do not envisage being dominant, but which an audience might take if it wants to resist the 'preferred' reading. 'Queer' readings of films, in which attention is drawn to a gay subtext, or overtly politicised readings, in which the ideology of a film is 'unmasked', are examples of oppositional reading.

By implication, the most likely reading of a film is going to be a 'negotiated' one, in which an audience will accommodate the dominant values offered, but without 'signing up' to them; Phillips's example of films, whose meanings are negotiated by the audience, are James Bond films, where audiences might, and often do, object to stereotyping of 'Bond girls' but put up with it because the films offer other pleasures – in narrative, action, spectacle, and corny humour.

The audience experience of a film is circumscribed by a great deal of activity by the film companies themselves in addition to the two hours of projected celluloid at the centre of the experience. Broadly called 'cinema culture', this comprises the ways in which films' meanings are circulated

'Cinema culture'

outside the cinema – in magazines, TV film programmes, film posters and trailers, the ways films are programmed in cinemas, for example in seasons and festivals, and in educational settings.

Thus the meanings associated with a film such as *Casablanca* are in a broader circulation than just those in the film itself. A later part of this section will consider the ways in which this film has been received over the years, but let's just say for the moment that anything written about the film, including this book, makes some contribution to *Casablanca* culture and the range of possible meanings the film has to offer.

In terms of audience theories, then, what you make of *Casablanca* will be determined by the following kinds of context, or 'determinant':

■ Whether you see the film in a cinema, or at least on a big screen, maybe at a film society. The difference that screen size makes will be explored in the section on spectatorship.

■ The context for viewing the film – it might be part of a course, like A Level, or part of a Humphrey Bogart season on television.

■ Whether you are seeing the film for the first time, now, in 2000, or whether you saw it when it came out in 1942.

■ Your social, cultural, political, and sexual orientation. The film's portrayal of the Nazi officers may make you feel uncomfortable if you are German; you may enjoy Captain Renault's character as high camp; you may resist Rick's hard-boiled cynicism as a crude macho posture.

'Cinema culture' is the business of circulating meanings and values associated with films across other media; however, films can circulate meanings within and between themselves, with no seeming contact with the outside world. The name for this cross-referencing, where films seem to 'talk to each other' is 'intertextuality'. One of the sources of *Casablanca*'s potency is that it occupies a central place in a dense network of intertextual reference.

intertextuality

Because media products – particularly films – are produced collaboratively, they are in effect a melange of quotes, references, ideas and images which

intertextuality

find echoes in other texts and products. They are microcosms of language itself, in that words, or units of meaning, carry with them the traces of long use, of currency. When elements of texts can be sourced to other texts, these references come under the rubric 'intertextuality'.

Casablanca is dense with intertextual references. First of all, there are a range of precursors for the film. The most significant is a French film called *Pepe le Moko* (1937), which starred Jean Gabin – in some ways an earlier French version of Humphrey Bogart. In fact, it is claimed that Pepe itself was based on *Scarface*, a Howard Hawks's gangster film of 1932.

Like Bogart, Gabin plays a doomed loner, all at sea in the centre of a Moroccan city. Like Rick, Pepe is subject to a love he can't consummate, and is at odds with the dominant authorities. One of the differences between the outcomes of the two films is that unlike Rick, Pepe does not escape; his isolation is partly derived from the fact that he is a criminal, rather than driven to a single criminal act, like Rick. Pepe is doomed in a way that would not have been acceptable for an American audience; for the sake of the propagandist message, Rick must make a sacrifice, but not at this stage sacrifice his life.

Pepe was re-made by independent producer Walter Wanger in 1938 as *Algiers*, a pot-boiler melodrama starring Charles Boyar and Hedy Lamarr which saw some success. *Casablanca* was in many ways an attempt to reproduce the success of the previous film, which explains the change of title from the original stage play. When the Epstein twins pitched the script on Warner Bros's behalf to David Selznick, who 'owned' Ingrid Bergman as her agent, they ended up saying. 'Oh, hell, it's going to be a lot of shit like *Algiers*.'

Films do not just steal or borrow references from other films; they themselves become a part of our cultural vocabulary. It is interesting to trace how this has happened to *Casablanca* – how it has continued to resonate since it was made.

Warner Bros in a belated attempt to cash in on the growth of television, turned some of their most popular films into TV series, and *Casablanca* was one of these. Inevitably, perhaps, the series was a flop; the peculiar potency of a film can be identified in its translation to TV programme. For

Alain Delon's
'look-alike' appearance
in *Le Samourai*

Casablanca, the power of the film is in the central personas and performances of Bogart and Bergman, and in the singularity of Rick's sacrifice. In the TV series the cast was new, and the character of Rick went on doing the noble thing week after week – which diluted the strength of his appeal.

Also in the 1950s, *Casablanca* morphed into a different kind of screen experience – the cult film. Long before *The Blues Brothers* (1980) or *The Rocky Horror Picture Show* (1975), *Casablanca* screenings were colonised by cult fans – dressing up as favourite characters, quoting lines of dialogue, shouting back at the screen.

Since then *Casablanca* has entered our everyday cultural vocabulary in sayings such as 'Here's looking at you, kid'; *Casablanca* has more entries than any other film in the *Oxford Modern Dictionary of Quotations*. Bogart's 'look' has been used – 'quoted' – almost as much as the dialogue, for example by Alain Delon in the 1967 film *Le Samourai*, and by a series of beer adverts in the 1980s.

The most famous after-echo of the film, and the reason why the most famous line in the film is so often misquoted, is Woody Allen's *Play it Again, Sam* (1972). In this, Allen plays the nerd role which he has become associated with, trying to seduce Diane Keaton. Allen seeks advice on macho behaviour from a Rick look-alike, dressed in trademark trench coat and wide-brimmed hat. 'Rick' advises him on one-liners and strategies for impressing his girl, and Allen is frequently, joyously, mystified that Rick's strategies seem to work. The film is at once a hymn to old-fashioned mores, as well as being a tongue-in-cheek laugh at them.

What Allen was doing, even then, was dramatising a crisis in male confidence about how to relate to the opposite sex; the result is both a retreat to a time of more certain gender relations, as well as a recognition that, like Sam, they no longer 'play'. Thus the central focus of *Casablanca* – the character of the hard-boiled but noble Rick – comes to signify almost its opposite – the impossibility of behaving like him in contemporary 1970s America.

Play it again, Sam: Woody Allen
seeks advice from a Rick look-alike

the film spectator

the film spectator

The other approach to the study of audience mentioned earlier is the study of the film spectator. Unlike audiences, the spectator is conceived as a single, solitary figure, maybe part of a group of viewers of a film, but once inside the cinema, essentially alone in their relationship to what is projected on screen.

The peculiar viewing conditions of cinema – in the dark, witnessing an enlarged version of the world, alongside people to whom we do not speak – have made it ripe for psychoanalytical theory to explore. The central processes – projection, and viewing without being watched back, or voyeurism – are potent metaphors in Freudian psychology.

Phillips's outline is that film as a system (or 'apparatus' in the more suggestive phrase) creates a position for the spectator to inhabit, a position which already determines the range of possible responses and engagement. Dominant cinema – what we think of as mainstream Hollywood – operates in such a way that we are bound into one mode of representation. As was mentioned in Style: Editing, the classic continuity system seeks invisibility, and similarly the apparatus of cinema space and projection discourages us from interacting, heckling, chatting, or even ignoring the images being presented.

As many film critics have made clear, the cinema apparatus effectively presents one view of the world. Laura Mulvey coined the phrase 'the male gaze' (see Cook, 1999 or 1994) to identify this; she argued that the 'eye' of the camera, operated by a man, and directed usually by a man, replicated a male viewing position in the cinema. Allied to this was the fact that the camera looked at women in ways different from men, often taking the point of view of a male character; women were thus the object of the 'male gaze'. This viewing position was replicated in the cinema, offering in effect the feeling for the spectator of being a 'peeping tom'.

In addition to describing a system of dominant kinds of 'look' in the cinema, spectator theory speculatively drew up some explanatory frameworks for why this kind of look works, founded on an understanding of pleasure and desire.

point of identification

Phillips identifies a range of pleasures. For the spectator, that is the individual, they are categorised as either sensory, emotional, or cognitive, and are differentiated from audience pleasures which he counts are anticipation, shared experience, and cultural exchange.

For *Casablanca*, it is possible to outline the several ways in which the film offers pleasures and, following Phillips, 'stages' our fantasies and desires.

One of the key tensions in pleasure and desire is between continuation and closure: the urge to postpone pleasure competes with the desire to complete it, a dynamic rooted for Freud in very early childhood. One of the key pleasures in *Casablanca* is in the 'staging' of this tension. Rick's transformation from isolationist to Allied partner, and Ilsa's flight from Casablanca are both large narrative movements which engage us in this way. In both cases we 'know' the outcome, but want to delay the moment of knowing for as long as the alternative gives us pleasure. Even on micro-narrative levels, we are teased with the gradual revelation of information, for example, the withholding of Ilsa's marriage to Laszlo from both us and Rick.

Rick is our point of identification in the film. We experience his journey, his hopes and desires, as our own – or at least as the ones privileged by the film. At the end we do not speculate about what happens next to Ilsa and Laszlo, but about Louis and Rick in Brazzaville. Indeed Warner Bros had already lined up the possibility of 'Brazzaville' being a sequel to the film.

The industry itself is often a magnifier of our desires and pleasures; as if they could not bear the film ending, Warner Bros executives planned for extra scenes to be added to the finale – of Allied soldiers landing in North Africa, of Renault and Bogart joining Free French soldiers.

Ilsa is a central figure for the engagement of desire in the film. Desire is structured around an absence – the thing sought will always be unattainable – and this is replicated in both our and Rick's engagement with her. One of the strengths of the Bergman persona is in her unavailability – a radiant beauty that seems unworldly, in fact ideally

the film spectator

suited to 'silver screen' projection. The attraction she projects is not erotic, but idealised, and the position of the spectator is thus like Rick, to adore but not possess.

The drawbacks of conceiving of spectatorship as gendered male are probably immediately apparent. Surely there are female spectating positions in the cinema? And surely there must be room for different male spectating positions, in line with understandings of audience? One felicitous but not totally satisfactory answer is that the female spectator is subjected to and inhabits the male spectating position, and identifies with the women objectified on-screen, as they share this common experience of being female.

The arguments and counter-arguments over spectatorship eventually became very arcane, but the dominant idea – that individuals watching the same films share something of the same experience and response, and have little control over it – is still powerful and important. Scholarship in film studies, however, has moved on to consider the responses of specific audiences to specific films in particular times and places.

bibliography

general film

Altman, Rick, *Film Genre,*
BFI, 1999
Detailed exploration of film genres

Bordwell, David, *Narration in the Fiction Film,* Routledge, 1985
A detailed study of narrative theory and structures

– – –, Staiger, Janet & Thompson, Kristin, *The Classical Hollywood Cinema: Film Style & Mode of Production to 1960,* Routledge, 1985; pbk 1995
An authoritative study of cinema as institution, it covers film style and production

– – – & Thompson, Kristin, *Film Art,* McGraw-Hill, 4th edn, 1993
An introduction to film aesthetics for the non-specialist

Branson, Gill & Stafford, Roy, *The Media Studies Handbook,* Routledge, 1996

Buckland, Warren, *Teach Yourself Film Studies,* Hodder & Stoughton, 1998
Very accessible, it gives an overview of key areas in film studies

Cook, Pam (ed.), *The Cinema Book,* BFI, 1994; 2nd edn 1999

Corrigan, Tim, *A Short Guide To Writing About Film,* HarperCollins, 1994
What it says: a practical guide for students

Dyer, Richard, *Stars,* BFI, 1979; 2nd edn 1998
A good introduction to the star system

Easthope, Antony, *Classical Film Theory,* Longman, 1993
A clear overview of recent writing about film theory

Hayward, Susan, *Key Concepts in Cinema Studies,* Routledge, 1996

Hill, John & Gibson, Pamela Church (eds), *The Oxford Guide to Film Studies,* Oxford University Press, 1998
Wide-ranging standard guide

Lapsley, Robert & Westlake, Michael, *Film Theory: An Introduction,* Manchester University Press, 1994

Maltby, Richard & Craven, Ian, *Hollywood Cinema,* Blackwell, 1995
A comprehensive work on the Hollywood industry and its products

Mulvey, Laura, 'Visual Pleasure and Narrative Cinema' (1974), in Visual and Other Pleasures, Indiana University Press, Bloomington, 1989
The classic analysis of 'the look' and 'the male gaze' in Hollywood cinema. Also available in numerous other edited collections

Nelmes, Jill (ed.), *Introduction to Film Studies,* Routledge, 1996; 2nd edn 1999
Deals with several national cinemas and key concepts in film study

Nowell-Smith, Geoffrey (ed.), *The Oxford History of World Cinema,* Oxford University Press, 1996
Hugely detailed and wide-ranging with many features on 'stars'

Thomson, David, *A Biographical Dictionary of the Cinema*, Secker & Warburg, 1975
Unashamedly driven by personal taste, but often stimulating

Truffaut, François, *Hitchcock*, Simon & Schuster, 1966, rev. edn, Touchstone, 1985
Landmark extended interview

Turner, Graeme, *Film as Social Practice*, 2nd edn, Routledge, 1993
Chapter four, 'Film Narrative', discusses structuralist theories of narrative

Wollen, Peter, *Signs and Meaning in the Cinema*, Viking, 1972
An important study in semiology

Readers should also explore the many relevant websites and journals. *Film Education* and *Sight and Sound* are standard reading.

Valuable websites include:

The Internet Movie Database at
http://uk.imdb.com

Screensite at
http://www.tcf.ua.edu/screensite/contents.html

The Media and Communications Site at the University of Aberystwyth at
http://www.aber.ac.uk/~dgc/welcome.html

There are obviously many other university and studio websites which are worth exploring in relation to film studies.

casablanca

Andrew, Geoff, *Directors A–Z: A Concise Guide to the Art of 250 Great Film Makers*, Prion Books, 1999

Barthes, Roland, (trans. A. Lavers) *Mythologies*, Paladin, 1989

Behlmer, Rudy (ed.), *Inside Warner Bros (1935–1951)*, Weidenfeld and Nicolson, 1986

Chatman, Seymour, *Story and Discourse: Narrative Structure in Fiction and Film*, Ithaca: Cornell University Press, 1978

Chion, Michel, *Audio-Vision: Sound on Screen*, Chichester: Columbia University Press, 1994

Eco, Umberto, 'Casablanca: Cult Movies and Intertextual Collage', in *Travels in Hyperreality*, Picador, 1987

Harmetz, Aljean, *Round Up the Usual Suspects: The Making of Casablanca*, Weidenfeld and Nicolson, 1993

Miller, Frank, *Casablanca: As Time Goes By*, Virgin Books, 1993

Ray, Robert B., *A Certain Tendency of the Hollywood Cinema 1930–1980*, Princeton, New Jersey: Princeton University Press, 1985

Robertson, James C., *The Casablanca Man: The Cinema of Michael Curtiz*, Routledge, 1993

Schatz, Thomas, *The Genius of the System: Hollywood Filmmaking in the Studio Era*, Faber and Faber, 1998

Sperber, A.M. and Lax, Eric, *Bogart*, Weidenfeld and Nicolson, 1997

Vogler, Christopher, *The Writer's Journey: Mythic Structure for Storytellers & screenwriters*, London: Boxtree, 1996

cinematic terms

auteur term used to describe a film director with a signature visual style, and whose films elaborate a coherent personal vision. Coined by French critics in the 1920s, and developed by a later generation who wrote for the journal *Cahiers du Cinema* into the 'politique des auteurs'

auteur theory see 'politique des auteurs', and 'auteur'

classic continuity editing see 'Realism' and 'editing'

classic Hollywood cinema/ classic Hollywood narrative a sample of films produced in Hollywood during the studio-system years and beyond, have been analysed by the critic David Bordwell (1985) and reduced to a specific pattern of form and style. The pattern is structured around seamless Realism in which the audience/spectator is prevented from leaving the diegetic world of the film until it is over.

The narrative follows a strict cause-and-effect logic, in which only events fitting the plot directly, and springing from earlier diegetic causes will figure at all. The narrative also follows the desires of single protagonists and their overcoming of obstacles. It ends in a strong closure, invariably a happy ending

diegetic time/diegetic sound the term diegetic refers to the world a film seeks to portray. It is most commonly used to refer to time in the film (to distinguish it from the time being experienced by the audience) and sound. Diegetic sound is any sound – sound effects, dialogue, or music – which has its source directly in the world of the film. Non-diegetic sound, therefore, is any sound sourced from outside – like voice-over, or soundtrack music

editing in addition to mise-en-scène, editing is the other system of meaning-making to come under film language. Editing is the mode by which diegetic time and space are represented – in the former, in the management of duration, order, and frequency of story events; and in the latter, through the construction of point of view and the montage of shots (see also montage editing, Realism)

expressionism/ expressionist see German Expressionism

film noir a label derived from the title of a series of American detective novels translated into French in the 1940s, and called either the 'Serie Noir', or more generally the 'roman noir', meaning 'dark novel'.

By the 1950s, the term had been appropriated by film critics in Europe and beyond to refer to a group of films – usually B movies – made by the Hollywood studio system between the mid-1940s and late 1950s.

The film noir was characterised by expressionist lighting and mise-en-scène, and reflected a nihilistic moral outlook. In terms of narrative and representation, they featured a 'doomed' central male protagonist who was seduced by a sexually aggressive 'femme fatale'. Identified in the 1950s, it has since become a model for subsequent film-makers

genre/genre theory an examination of films based on typologies of shared characteristics. Originally a theoretical approach which enabled critics to value and appreciate Hollywood studio films which had not been labelled as 'auteur' films. Key genres include the Western (the prototype genre for genre theory

cinematic terms

(see Altman, 1999, and Nelmes, 1996 for further reading), the musical and the gangster film.

There is some debate over whether the idea of genre originated with studios, or whether critics developed it themselves, after the films – under scrutiny – were made. Genre study is focused primarily on Hollywood films of the studio era, and so it has been suggested that what passes for genre study is really only the study of what is typical in classic Hollywood cinema

German Expressionism a movement in film-making in Germany in the 1920s. Aimed at reproducing and representing powerful emotion via cinematic means, its principal directors were Fritz Lang and F.W. Murnau. The movement influenced Hollywood films of the 1930s and 1940s, mainly because the leading directors and technicians of the movement moved to America to escape Nazi Germany

Hays Office (Hays Code) in 1922, the major Hollywood studios organised themselves into a cartel, represented by the Motion Picture Producers and Distributors of America (MPPDA). Its first head was ex-Republican senator Will Hays, who gave the office its more commonly used name.

In 1934, following pressure from political and religious groups agitating for censorship of films, the MPPDA published its own code of film-making practice – called the Motion Picture Production Code (MPPC). This quickly became known as the Hays Code. The code listed proscribed activities and behaviours – mostly criminal or sexual, or those which might offend religious or national groups

hegemony/hegemonic narrative hegemony is a term coined by the Italian Marxist Antonio Gramsci to describe the ways in which democratic societies manage to maintain the dominance of a set of ideas, values, and beliefs, while appearing to be open, pluralist, and consensual. The success of hegemony was that the dominant ideology would come to be seen as 'natural' or 'common-sense'.

A parallel to this process can be found in media products, especially mainstream films. The classic Hollywood film through its narrative, editing and mise-en-scène has come to be seen as the only 'natural' way of making films; anything different is by definition deviant, marginal, or oppositional. In line with the workings of hegemony, Hollywood has found itself able to absorb developments in film language and technology without being threatened

high–key/low–key lighting lighting can be characterised as one of three types: key lighting – direct light on to an object or person; 'fill' lighting – where a general space is lit to fill it out, or give it the appearance of three dimensionality; and 'backlighting' – where a light is shone behind an object to give it an ominous or mysterious silhouette look.

Key lighting can either be high, as in the lighting of a star's face to look glossy, glamorous, or luminous, or low, to create a shadowy or mysterious atmosphere. Hollywood's 'Realist' cinema tends to light a scene just enough to appear 'real'; 'expressionist' lighting abandons the realist aesthetic in favour of high contrast

cinematic terms

Hollywood studio system film production in Hollywood became organised along 'systematic' lines as early as 1913 when Thomas Ince pioneered the 'factory' method of production. Essentially, films were made on a conveyor-belt system with personnel – writers, directors, cast and crew, editors and musicians – doing their specific jobs and then moving on to another picture. In effect, this enabled a studio to put out a film a week at the height of production. Because this system was similar to that of car production pioneered by Henry Ford, it has been called 'Fordist'

ideology a system of ideas, beliefs and values shared by a group of people with common habits and interests. Originally conceived by Karl Marx as a way of describing the relationship between ideas, power, and social groups, it has moved beyond the function of describing dominant ideas and values. The Marxist conception of ideology was developed in Gramsci's notion of hegemony

major film studios in the 1930s and 1940s, Hollywood – and world – film production was dominated by five major studios, each of whom made, sold, and exhibited their own films. In that sense, the definition of a *major* studio is that it integrated production, distribution, and exhibition. Vertical integration was challenged in the US courts in 1948 as being monopolistic, and the studios – slowly – divested themselves of their cinema chains.

In 1942, the five majors were MGM, Paramount, Warner Bros, 20th Century Fox and RKO. In addition, there were three 'little' majors, who did not actually own cinemas – Columbia, Universal, and United Artists. Essentially, these eight, as well as Disney, are still the major players today

melodrama a problematic term with a range of interpretations. Used by the film press and the studios in the 1930s and 1940s to label films in which powerful emotions were at the core – something akin to the current video-store category 'Drama' – although adventure stories were also considered to be melodramatic.

Later the term came to be equated with films made specifically for women, which featured female protagonists and 'domestic' narratives. Thus, *Casablanca, Mildred Pierce* and *All That Heaven Allows* can be called melodramas, but for very different reasons

mise-en-scène in French, this literally means 'what's put in the scene'. It covers the content and composition of the *shot*, which is the basic unit of meaning in the cinema. Categories under which to describe content and composition include setting, costume, props; body language, facial expression and gesture of actors; the formal framing, composition, and choreography of elements in the shot; and the cinematography – the use of camera and lighting.

More than this, the focus on the mise-en-scène as the bearer of meaning constituted for the critic Andre Bazin in itself an aesthetic of cinema; for him it meant the idea that the director could most clearly express artistic vision and intent through the shot, especially if, as in the studio system, both scriptwriting and editing were out of their control

cinematic terms

montage editing a system devised by Soviet film-makers in the 1920s whereby a sequence of images might be put together to construct arguments and ideas as much as to propel a narrative

politique des auteurs a position developed by critics writing for the French film journal *Cahiers du Cinema* in the 1950s, headed by Andre Bazin. Its function was to celebrate directors working in the Hollywood studio system whose work was defined by a signature visual style. Directors given this label included Orson Welles, Alfred Hitchcock, John Ford and Howard Hawks. In America, the film critic Andrew Sarris picked up the phrase and extended it into a theoretical position celebrating the Hollywood studio product as the most artistically – and commercially – significant in the world. Sarris cited *Casablanca* as 'perhaps the one great exception to the auteur theory'

Realism Susan Hayward (1996) distinguishes between two types of Realism – 'aesthetic' and 'seamless'. Aesthetic realism refers to film-making where effort is taken to reproduce life/reality as it is – as in the documentary movements in Britain, Italy, Germany and France this century. The second type, 'seamless' Realism, refers to the dominant – Hollywood – mode of cinema, in which the system is structured around the desire to render technique and production invisible. Thus a grammar of film language – in mise-en-scène, editing, and sound – evolved in the first half of this century which strove to disguise itself. Not crossing the line, shot/reverse shot photography, graphic matches, and justified cutting

are all techniques which hide the fact that the film is being 'cut' at all

spectator/spectatorship a term – and theory – used to describe the singular experience of watching a film, derived from psychoanalytic theories and categories. Distinguished from sociological approaches to the study of the cinema experience which focus on plural audiences and diverse responses.

Spectatorship theories are derived from the understanding that the cinema experience is close to the dream state – images are screened in the dark to a largely passive audience – and thus parallel to unconscious experiences of desire and pleasure.

Spectatorship has been gendered as male, because of the 'male gaze' wherein the whole cinema apparatus – director, cameraman, and actors – is constructed around the look of men focused on woman/women as object

structuralism this is derived from a theory of language developed by the Swiss linguist Ferdinand de Saussure, which became a programmatic method for examining cultural products/texts in the 1960s and 1970s. Saussure's idea about language was that it was a system where meaning was a product of binary – oppositional – relationships. It was picked up by among others, anthropologist Claude Levi-Strauss and by Roland Barthes

Its influence on film study is in its application to narrative – for example, how Western narratives are a 'managed' sets of opposites like male/ female; civilisation/wilderness; justice/law; inside/outside. It also found applications in the study of genre

credits

production company
Warner Brothers

producer
Hal B. Wallis

director
Michael Curtiz

writers
Julius J. and Phillip G. Epstein,
and Howard Koch
(based on the play *Everybody
Comes to Rick's* by Murray Burnett
and Joan Alison)

photography
Arthur Edeson

music
Max Steiner

editor
Owen Marks

art direction
Carl Jules Weyl

set design
George James Hopkins

music direction
Leo Forbstein

orchestrations
Hugo Friedhofer

gowns
Orry-Kelly

make-up
Perc Westmore

special effects
Lawrence Butler, Willard Van Enger

montages
Don Siegel, James Leicester

technical adviser
Robert Aisner

music/lyrics
'Knock on Wood', 'That's What
Noah Done', 'Muse's Call',
M. K. Jerome, Jack Scholl

'As Time Goes By', Herman Hupfeld

cast
Richard 'Rick' Blaine –
Humphrey Bogart

Ilsa Lund Laszlo – Ingrid Bergman

Victor Laszlo – Paul Henreid

Captain Louis Renault –
Claude Rains

Major Heinrich Strasser –
Conrad Veidt

Senor Ferrari – Sydney Greenstreet

Ugarte – Peter Lorre

Carl, Headwaiter – S.Z. Sakall

Yvonne – Madeleine LeBeau

Sam – Dooley Wilson

Annina Brandel – Joy Page

Berger – John Qualen